YOU ARE A MOGUL

HOW TO

DO THE **IMPOSSIBLE,**

DO IT **YOURSELF,**

AND DO IT **NOW**

TIFFANY PHAM

SIMON & SCHUSTER

NEW YORK   LONDON   TORONTO   SYDNEY   NEW DELHI

Simon & Schuster
1230 Avenue of the Americas
New York, NY 10020

First Simon & Schuster hardcover edition September 2018

SIMON & SCHUSTER and colophon are registered
trademarks of Simon & Schuster, Inc.

For information about special discounts for bulk purchases,
please contact Simon & Schuster Special Sales at 1-866-506-1949
or business@simonandschuster.com.

The Simon & Schuster Speakers Bureau can bring authors to your live event.
For more information or to book an event contact the
Simon & Schuster Speakers Bureau at 1-866-248-3049
or visit our website at www.simonspeakers.com.

Interior design by Ruth Lee-Mui

Manufactured in the United States of America

10   9   8   7   6   5   4   3   2   1

Library of Congress Cataloging-in-Publication Data

ISBN 978-1-5011-9185-5
ISBN 978-1-5011-9187-9 (ebook)

To my father, mother, sister, Kym, and brother, David,

for being the most amazing, supportive family.

Thank you for believing in me and us every step of the way.

We are where we are today because of you.

CONTENTS

You are not just a woman.

You are fierce.

You are bold.

You are unique.

You are brilliant.

You are motivated.

You are driven.

You are empowering.

You are inspiring.

You are a mogul.

INTRODUCTION

Four years ago, I sat in my bedroom and began creating a digital platform for women across the world. I wasn't outrageously ambitious about the numbers of women I would initially reach. I was a twenty-seven-year-old business school grad, working three jobs at once. But I decided to try to build this idea I had on my own, in the hours I had to myself after my jobs were finished each night. Over a period of months, I taught myself how to code, showing my fledgling site to a few people for feedback. And then, I sent it out into the world, unsure of what its impact and reach might be. But I was hopeful it could become a vehicle to show women exactly how much we are capable of—that when we come together, we can rise faster, go farther, and truly change the world.

That platform ended up becoming Mogul, the company that I now run today, with offices in New York City, San Francisco, and Paris. One of the largest platforms for women worldwide, Mogul reaches millions of people across 196 countries through its mobile app, the web, email, social media, books, TV, films, and events. Thousands of jobs are posted on Mogul each day. It offers award-winning Unconscious Bias, Inclusive Leadership, and Gender Equity trainings. It addresses safety at work through cutting-edge harassment reporting tools. Fortune 1000 companies are pledging to Mogul that they will improve how they present women in their communications. For every dollar Mogul earns, the company provides free educational resources to women in need through international partners such as the United Nations.

And though we find ourselves today at the pinnacle of success, it didn't come easy, and it didn't happen overnight. My journey, and the journey of Mogul, was fueled by unending determination and resilience, no matter how challenging the circumstances; a perpetual desire to learn more, become more; and the knowledge that, step-by-step, you can do anything you want to do and be anything you want to be.

So if you've ever been laid off, shut down, told no, doubted yourself, or been doubted, then look no further. Welcome to our Mogul world, where all of that is about to change. **It doesn't matter how old you are or where you are starting from—anyone can become a mogul.** Especially you.

If you're thinking that it's not possible because you just don't fit the powerful businessman stereotype, spoiler alert: that's not what a mogul is or looks like anymore.

It's true. Before I launched Mogul, when you Googled the word "mogul," the top search results were links to businessmen like Warren Buffett and Rupert Murdoch.

But, today, when you Google the word "mogul," we are the number-one search result. A community of women across the globe, connecting, sharing, and striving to change the world. We are redefining the word for the next generation of girls to know that they, too, can be moguls.

We all have the power to create something great, whether it is a social enterprise, a nonprofit, beautiful artwork that inspires the world, or technology that makes people's lives easier. I share my story and the story of Mogul so that you can apply every lesson I have learned to your life today, accelerating your own growth, personally and professionally, and reaching your goals sooner than you thought would ever be possible.

And while I may seem polished from the outside in my heels and power dress, know that I'm not all business. Deep down, I'm still the underdog, the one who didn't believe in herself, the shy girl who moved from Paris, France, to Plano, Texas, struggling to learn a new language and adapt to a new culture all at once. But through the years, I've learned to step up to the moment, and to not let self-doubt hold me back. Though I've been compared to Fortune 500 CEOs, that's just not me. I'm used to marching to the beat of my own drum, and to being the youngest in the room, the only female in the room, or the only Asian in the room. I've figured out how to not let that or anything keep me from accomplishing what I set my mind to. Even if others said no along the way, I never let that stop me. I've consistently made choices that led me to overcome obstacles and achieve new heights much faster than expected. Choices that I want to share with you, so that you can learn to do the same. You'll also hear from ten of my friends and the most powerful moguls worldwide, including Nina García, Star Jones, Rebecca Minkoff, and more. They share their personal stories and insights, so that you can adopt their learning, too.

Before we get started, a brief disclaimer: I have tried to the best of my ability to recall everything that happened in these pages accurately. But I am human, just like you. I might have gotten a date slightly out of order. I surely hope I didn't misremember a name or memory. But know that this book is my best attempt to put forth the truth of my life, and the creation of Mogul, while respecting certain people's privacy.

And know this, too: within you lie the courage and confidence to do what hasn't been done before, a voice that we desperately need to hear, and the ability to see problems and devise innovative solutions in a way that can truly impact the world.

Becoming a mogul isn't about becoming rich, although that is a pleasant side effect. It's about thinking for yourself, identifying and embracing your unique strengths and passions, and using those to make the world a better place.

When we fully step into our power, there is no predicting the heights we can reach.

1 PINPOINT YOUR PASSIONS

In many ways, I've known what I wanted to do with my life since I was fourteen years old. That was the year that the course of my life changed, as you'll learn in the pages that follow. The events that took place then led me to decide, at that time, that I would do everything I could to help others. I would dedicate my life to not only showing others what they could strive for, but helping them to achieve it. That goal became a guiding force for me, a promise to myself that I aimed to keep as I went forth in the world.

Pinpointing that passion early, and having something that I was doggedly pursuing from the age of fourteen, allowed me to rise and become a mogul at a young age. I envisioned the course that I wanted for my career, and said yes to opportunities that I thought might help me get to my goal. I was continually focused on this goal, even though I didn't know exactly what the path might look like. In fact, it was that willingness to not know the exact path that allowed me to get there faster than anyone could have predicted.

How did I get to be so driven? I had powerful influences throughout my life that shaped me to dream big, learn everything I could, and strive for excellence. Those influences were the fuel that kept me going. They reminded me of what was possible.

Whether you're fourteen or forty, it's never too early or too late to dream big. When you have a passion to keep you going, and role models to inspire you, there is no limit to what you can do.

FAIL FORWARD

I was born in Paris, France, to Vietnamese and Chinese parents, and thus grew up speaking a combination of languages, including French and Vietnamese. My early years were idyllic. My older sister, Kym, younger brother, David, and I spent our days riding our red tricycles around the fenced-in courtyard of our house, eating buttered crêpes on the Champs-Élysées, and skipping by the Château de Vincennes. Like my favorite scenes from *Amélie*, but with more phở.

Then, when I was ten, my family moved to Plano, Texas, and suddenly, my life transformed from a scene from *Amélie* to an episode of *Friday Night Lights*. It was a land of pickup trucks, McDonald's, and American football. And we loved it, too, despite the differences.

I remember my childhood in Texas fondly now, but at the time, I did worry whether I could ever fit in. Thanks to my startlingly bright braces, thick-rimmed glasses, and bowl cut, I'd say my worries weren't completely unfounded.

Plus, I was extremely quiet in school. Not just because of my innate shyness, but because I did not speak English well. I didn't know how to communicate with my teachers, let alone my classmates. My mother worried about me as she watched me come home from school and color, instead of doing my homework. I still couldn't read any of the worksheets I was sent home with.

But even though those first few months were challenging, I would later see that time of ongoing transition as a pivotal part of my story.

In their younger years, my parents had often spent entire days at the theater in France, where they showed screening after screening of black-and-white American classics. This was the genesis of their love affair with America, and their appreciation of classic American cinema continued when we moved to the States. We often had Turner Classic Movies on after school. My parents knew that the more we were exposed to the language, the quicker we would learn. As a result, I grew up watching women like Audrey Hepburn and Marilyn Monroe show me how elegant, charming, but also powerful women could be. And while I slowly began to pick up English, and engage more with my classmates and teachers, I was also glimpsing how powerful media could be for learning, for showing you what was possible. And I never forgot that feeling.

I'm thankful now for how those early years of having to adjust to a new language and a new culture allowed me to learn how to belong anywhere, to be curious about new places and new ideas, and to be ready and willing to incorporate new perspectives into my growing worldview. Because to be a mogul, you have to see outside your current situation, and be willing to engage with the world, arms wide-open to accept its lessons, its differing beliefs, and its varied paths to influence and impact. The world is the greatest school there is, if you are open to its education.

My father and mother were exemplary role models in this regard. Despite the fact that they had to rebuild their lives not once (when they immigrated to France), but twice when they then moved the family to America, I never saw my father and mother discouraged. I saw them push forward, always, no matter what difficulty lay in their path, seeing each new challenge as an opportunity to learn something new. Even as they had to find new jobs and new homes as we traversed the world, they never let anything defeat them. All for the family. They embraced change and new experiences, and they raised their children to be truly engaged with the world around them.

In time, with each new city I moved to, and each new job I took on, whenever I would face challenges, my father would remind me, "There is no such thing as failure as long as you are moving forward. As long as you're learning, in the end, you're succeeding. True failure is not doing, not trying. So fail forward, and you'll always find yourself where you are supposed to be."

My father, in particular, was relentlessly curious and constantly challenging himself to do new things. That passion for learning was passed on to his children. My parents let my siblings and me try anything we might be interested in. If we didn't like it, we could move on to another activity. If we loved it, we were encouraged to become the best we could be. There were probably a half-dozen interests that I left behind before discovering my love of Tae Kwon Do, lacrosse, violin, and piano.

On the way to various practices and lessons, in our red Nissan minivan, my father would play audiotapes by Dale Carnegie, the author of *How to Stop Worrying and Start Living*. Dale's voice was the soundtrack to my childhood. How lessons written in the 1940s by a sixty-year-old man from Missouri felt so relevant to my life at the time, I don't know. But whenever my father was driving, Dale's tapes were playing in the cassette player, and I loved listening. Just like my father, Dale taught resilience, positive thinking, and self-improvement.

I grew up with this unstoppable spirit and dedicated determination as the backbone of my family. And just like certain traits can be passed down from generation to generation, so can passion, so can curiosity, so can kindness and resilience and perseverance. That belief in forward momentum, risk-taking, and the constant pursuit of your dreams, cultivated in me early on, was the foundation for me to become a mogul today.

Building Resilience

It's not always easy to buy into the idea of failing forward. But if you can, like me, learn early on to stay focused on the forward momentum, you'll build incredible resilience that will serve you in all areas of your life. Look back on your life, at moments where you felt like you failed. Now think about what lessons you took away and what doors were opened because of that failure. You tried, you learned. And odds are, you became that much better because of it. Whether it is a job you didn't get or a college that didn't accept you or an opportunity that seemed to slip through your fingers, I, like my father, have come to see that it is not about the missed opportunity, but what you did in the wake of said failure. If you ultimately found a different job, enrolled in a different school, or searched for a similar opportunity, you could still get to just as great of a place as if life had gone entirely according to plan, if not better.

Any time you feel like you failed, exercise your resilience. If you can just stay focused on all the assets you gained and momentum you now have for moving forward, you'll find that in the end, with perseverance, that failure will turn into a success story.

DON'T BE SATISFIED WITH THE STATUS QUO

By the time I reached high school, I had finally learned English well enough that my accent was receding. My grades at the time were good, but they weren't stellar. I was too busy with the social scene and making it through each day to dedicate myself to studying. I would never earn a score of 100 percent on anything. I would often get an A-minus, and at a very competitive public school, this was far from the top of the class.

My freshman year, I had a math teacher who would have his students grade each other's work, so that at night, he wouldn't have to grade all thirty papers.

In that class I sat behind a girl named Diane. She was kind and soft-spoken. When we would trade papers, and I would grade her work, she always got a 100 percent. Every time. She would then pass my paper back to me and I would have scored a 92 or 93.

As the days went by and this kept happening, something took root in me. Why was I settling? Clearly, a 100 percent *was* possible. If I was going to put in the time to complete the work, why not put in that little bit of extra effort if it meant a perfect score? Why was I selling myself short?

I made the decision, *From now on, if ever I'm going to do something, I might as well try to do the very best I can at it.*

So I started to study. Every night I would sit down to my math assignments and commit to getting a 100 percent myself. I wanted to be more like Diane.

And it worked. I started getting 100s. As my grades improved, Diane would turn around and hand my paper back to me, smiling. She could tell something had changed in me, and she was rooting for me. She knew that me trying to do my best didn't diminish her. We could both excel.

Diane and I soon became best friends and would spend hours studying at each other's houses on the weekends. Together, we were eventually ranked in the top 1 percent of our class of more than a thousand students. A decade and a half later, I was a bridesmaid in her wedding. We still talk and laugh every day.

This was a pivotal experience in my life because Diane made it apparent to me, at the ripe age of fourteen, that I had two options: I could push myself beyond what I thought was possible and perform in ways I couldn't have imagined, or I could be satisfied with the status quo.

Because of her example, I decided to strive for excellence. And this philosophy began to impact other areas of my life. I infused passion into everything I did, instead of settling for things as they were. Step-by-step, through incremental daily progress. I began to train night and day for my black belt in Tae Kwon Do. I practiced drill after drill to make the varsity lacrosse team. And I rehearsed for hours until I made first violin in orchestra and was awarded top honors in piano.

That was my first lesson in learning that achieving the "impossible" is usually possible with hard work and unwavering dedication. When you set yourself up for success, you often surpass what once seemed impossible. Not just for grades or accolades, but because there is no better feeling than doing your best, whatever your best might be.

Right there are the seeds to what I would eventually create with Mogul. **You can be more than what you believed you could be when you find examples to follow, and sometimes those examples are sitting right in front of you.**

FOLLOW IN HER FOOTSTEPS

I had another such role model for excellence in my grandmother.

I had grown up listening to our family's stories of all my grandmother had accomplished in Asia, anecdotes of her courage, kindness, and endless generosity toward those around her. My grandmother was a force of nature, a bold pioneer. She was among the first women to drive a car in Vietnam. She didn't let restrictions hold her back. At a time when other young women around the world suffered from lack of opportunities, she owned businesses across industries and would provide jobs to others in need. She was beloved by all and committed to helping the masses. She was a maverick of her time and an inspiration to me, as well as to the family that surrounded her. It was a beautiful portrait of what a woman could be. She was a mogul in every sense of the word.

Once we moved to Texas, we were able to more easily visit with my grandmother, who had also moved to the United States by this time. I'd heard about her my entire life, and it was amazing to finally spend time with her. She was no longer just a legend to me but a flesh-and-blood person, a loving matriarch who would do anything for her children and grandchildren. Being able to see this woman in person, and witness her kindness and generosity, is one of the most powerful memories of my childhood. In my young and impressionable mind, it made sense to me then how my father had grown to be such a strong, kind, and giving man; and why he cherished those same qualities in my wonderful mother. I so wanted to be like them.

Sadly, within several years, my grandmother passed away. I remember vividly the moment when my father let me know.

After initial moments of silence in our house, I went into a small closet and curled up on the floor in the darkness. And as sadness washed over me, I remember saying: *I promise I will make you proud. I promise I will make my parents proud. I promise.*

In that moment, I vowed that I would do everything I could to follow in my grandmother's footsteps. I, too, wanted to be a pioneer, shattering people's expectations and being a role model to others. I, too, wanted to provide opportunities to those who needed them, and break down barriers. I would dedicate every waking moment to this goal. No matter how challenging.

I was still a teenager—braces, glasses, bowl cut, and all. I didn't know exactly how I would accomplish that goal, or what it might look like once I did. But from that moment forward, my mission was set, and the course of my life was changed.

Creating Paths of Possibility

Everyone needs an example to follow. A guide for the way forward. A trailblazer who isn't afraid to go where no woman has gone before. Women need to see other women being successful, in positions of power, and having a global impact. Together, we create paths of possibility for those that come after us.

Becoming a mogul means realizing that you are not alone in this world. That there are people who have gone before you to show you the way. Find others who inspire you, who keep you focused on what is possible. Vow to follow in their footsteps, so that others can follow in yours. That commitment will keep you going even during the hard days ahead.

BE FLEXIBLE YET STRATEGIC

By the time I applied to colleges, I was beginning to crystallize how this goal might materialize. I wrote in my essays about how my family inspired and influenced me and reiterated my promise to follow in my grandmother's footsteps. With each paragraph written, my dream began to take shape. Seeing how a role model had given me so much to strive for and allowed me the opportunity to dream, I vowed to create a company that would provide such examples to other women worldwide. I knew that it was vital to showcase the accomplishments and inherent strength of women, in order to enable the next generation of girls to know they could be bold and daring, and could pursue positions of impact and influence.

With each of those applications and essays, I developed a storyline for my life; a narrative that had a beginning, middle, and hoped-for ending that likely allowed me to stand out from the crowd. Whether you think about it this way or not, every application you fill out, every job interview you walk into, and every resume you send is a story of who you are and all the things you bring to the table. And you have to sell that story. Yes, you have to sell yourself: showcase the fact that you are going places, with or without them, and it will truly set you apart. This is an incredibly powerful tool for achieving the impossible.

I applied to four schools, including Yale and Stanford, without ever visiting their campuses. I was hesitant to spend my parents' hard-earned money traveling to visit the campuses, in case I didn't get in. As the months wore on, large envelopes finally arrived in our mailbox. I had been admitted to each one on scholarship. My father and mother wept with joy at the discovery. I had largely kept the application process to myself, not wanting to disappoint anyone else if it came to that. So when they opened the envelopes with me, one by one, it was quite the surprise.

I had dreamed of attending Yale during hours watching *Gilmore Girls*. I admired their brightest student, Rory Gilmore—who didn't have to be the loudest in the room to be the smartest in the room. She had a quiet confidence and lofty ambitions that she wouldn't lower for anyone (remember how she said she wanted to be Christiane Amanpour?). But when April of my senior year arrived and college decisions were becoming due, I was suddenly drawn to the idea of playing lacrosse at Stanford. My parents, meanwhile, were happy to support me no matter what I decided, though in their hearts, I knew they hoped I would select my first love.

Fairly certain I would attend Stanford, I decided to attend their Admitted Students' Weekend—the same weekend as my senior prom.

It wasn't an easy decision. There was a huge part of me that did not want to miss out on this pivotal part of American high school culture. I wondered whether I would always look back and feel a gaping hole at the center of my high school experience. But I think, even then, I knew that there was so much life ahead of me, so much of my future that would be determined by the decision of where I went to college. So I helped as my friends tried on dresses and cheered others on as they accepted dates, and I tried to stay focused on where I was going, on the future I was building.

My father flew to California with me. But as soon as I walked on campus, something felt off. Or rather, everything felt right to the point of feeling wrong. I felt such a sense of familiarity with the weather, the attire, the students I met. I didn't feel afraid, like I would be pushing myself beyond my comfort zone.

On the final day of Admitted Students' Weekend, my father and I were in the souvenir shop, buying Stanford T-shirts for the rest of the family before flying home. When we exited the shop, my father turned to me and, smiling, handed me a check for the document fee that would confirm my spot at Stanford. "This is a gift for you, from your mother and me."

I looked at him gratefully for a moment, then surprised even myself by saying, "Actually—I think I need to attend Yale."

My father exclaimed joyfully, while simultaneously being in shock. Here we were in California, having missed my prom—the event every senior had been looking forward to all year—so that I could get started on my time at Stanford. I must be mistaken.

But I knew I wasn't. I needed to attend Yale, to travel to the cold Northeast and be among buildings and people so different from what I had known before that I would have to confront any fears and trepidations. The environment, the culture would be so different that it would stretch me, embolden me to do more of the unthinkable.

I watched my father as he ripped up the check he had written, and when we got back to Texas that night, I mailed in my acceptance to Yale.

I trusted my gut then, as I still do now. It hasn't failed me yet.

All of my friends were shocked when I told them the news. And I was surprised, too. **But when you are willing to let go of your hard and fast notions of where life is supposed to take you, you open up to all the other opportunities that might be right around the corner.**

The truth is, flexibility is one of the greatest skills you can develop early on. I'm sure I don't have to tell you that the corporate landscape is changing, and very few of us will work for one company forever. Instead, more and more people are pursuing what journalist Farai Chideya calls "the episodic career." There is no longer one road map for a good life, personally or professionally. And while that provides for greater freedom to find our way, we have to learn to be as agile as the GPS on our phones: recalculating our route, our wants, our actions, sometimes a dozen times a day.

We live in a time when there is no longer one path to success. But that means that you should be always checking in with what feels right, true, and authentic for you. What do you want? What do you love? Where does your passion truly lie?

So here's a guideline that has been helpful for me as I navigate the twists and turns of life that don't always go the way you planned: **Be flexible but strategic.** Know what you want. Know where you want to end up. But don't get stuck thinking that the path to get there is set in stone. Set your destination, but be adaptable in what route you take. I use this approach when I travel as well. I have often been on planes to Oslo, or Dubai, or Panama City, with nothing but a list of spots that I definitely want to visit; I won't have a firm itinerary, filled to the brim with plans that prevent me from the fun side trips that are often the most rewarding and exciting part of the trip. There will be a cool-looking alleyway that could lead you to the kind of experience you are craving. If you only think there is one path to your goal, you're going to find yourself frustrated by how long that narrow road seems, and passing up opportunities that could take you exactly where you hope to go.

I've tried to be someone who says yes to many things, looking for different ways that that side trip or that unexpected opportunity, or job, might enable me to learn more, stretch me further, enable me to develop the relationships and skill sets to move faster toward my goals. I call these moments "accelerators." They are choices that I made, and experiences that I had, which catapulted me to the next level. In my early years, these accelerators helped me develop my passions and home in on what I truly loved to do. Later in my life, I focused on accelerators that would allow me to build skill sets that I would need in the job I knew I wanted to pursue. But the willingness to be open to opportunities along the way, flexible yet strategic, has been one of the most important accelerators on my career path.

Create Your Storyline

I was lucky enough to determine a storyline for myself at an early age, but it is never too late to stop and think about the story you want to tell. What problem is it that you are trying to solve? What is the one passion that drives all the various jobs that you've embarked upon thus far? Find a way to describe your career path—even if it has been nontraditional—as part of a storyline that has an interesting and purposeful narrative. It will not only help you on applications and job interviews, but also might help you as you try to make decisions about what steps to take next. Where are you trying to end up? What is the ending of your story? And what could you do next to get you there faster?

SOLVE THE PROBLEM YOURSELF

Your future will be born from the opportunities you take advantage of today. And while the specific ones that present themselves to you can depend on where you were born, the family you grew up in, and what rights, privileges, and experiences you have been given, there are countless opportunities that you can go after yourself. You don't have to wait around for them.

As my good buddy Dale Carnegie says (and I've updated on his behalf): "The [woman or] man who grasps an opportunity as it is paraded before [her or] him, nine times out of ten makes a success, but the [woman or] man who makes [her or] his own opportunities is, barring an accident, a sure-fire success."

I learned this firsthand my sophomore year at Yale. During my freshman year, I had struggled to find my place on campus. I had insisted on New Haven, after all, because it would force me to face a very different culture from that in Plano or Paris. I was up for the challenge. But navigating my new life on campus was more than I had bargained for. It took me that entire first year to push past this struggle, constantly doubting that I could ever be as smart or as talented as my classmates at Yale. As a result, that first year, I never raised my hand in class. I was close with my roommates, but struggled to meet anyone apart from the other students in Branford, my residential college.

When I got back to campus my sophomore year, I vowed to not allow another year to go by without taking steps toward getting involved in something, somehow. Soon thereafter, I found my opening: I joined the board for the Asian American Students Alliance—as their webmaster.

At our first board meeting, the discussion centered on a racist cartoon that had been printed in the previous week's issue of *The Yale Herald.* The other board members were livid, threatening to hold a protest outside.

Meanwhile, I flipped to the back cover of the newspaper and found a full-page advertisement announcing, in bright green, that *The Yale Herald* was recruiting for a financial analyst.

That's when it occurred to me. Instead of holding a protest outside, what if we could fix the problem from the inside?

My father had always taught me to be a doer: in difficult circumstances, try to resolve the issue at hand through problem-solving and action, not just discussion. Thus, while AASA continued to discuss how to address this cartoon, I was suddenly considering joining the newspaper.

I realized that if I joined and thus diversified their staff, I could help ensure they would not print a racist cartoon again.

I emailed the *Yale Herald* publisher that night, and to my delight, she immediately set up a meeting for the next day.

As I sat down with Jane, the publisher, inside local favorite the Buttery, I learned that it wasn't just that *The Yale Herald* lacked a diverse staff; they lacked a complete business team. There were just two people essentially running the newspaper. And the racist cartoon was the least of their issues. Due to mismanagement from prior years, the newspaper was in significant debt, debt that was increasing with each printed issue. The school was keeping the paper afloat but at a significant loss.

I was an economics major, so helping the newspaper's staff figure out their finances would be an interesting challenge for me, and a way to get involved in publishing. They were thrilled to add me to the team; they handed over their books, and essentially trusted me to start pulling them out of their dire situation.

This was my first crash course in company management: a company must succeed on all fronts to become a success. You can have the best content in the world, but if your company isn't financially sustainable, you aren't going to be around for long. For the most part, the newspaper staff focused on content, and getting the paper produced week after week. They ran a few ads each week, but they were from Yale organizations and brought in little revenue. *The Yale Herald* was distributed for free, so the only way to bring in more money was to sell more ads.

Now, if Jane had sent me a job description of the financial analyst role at the newspaper, I doubt it would have said anything about selling advertising. **But if you want to get ahead, you can't simply fulfill the job description. You have to do more than what is expected—for everyone's benefit, and for your growth, too.** In other words, if we were going to save the newspaper, then I had to roll up my sleeves and do whatever it was that needed to get done. No questions asked. Immediately. Even if that meant doing something I had never done before: selling door-to-door.

Over the course of the next few months, I raced to speak with local businesses that might be trying to attract a collegiate clientele. One of the first places I stopped at was called York Street Noodle House. It was a cozy, delicious Asian restaurant that had just recently opened on campus and that I thought might be perfect for my first pitch. When I walked in, I asked to speak to the manager, Soraya. As I got her attention, I made a personal appeal, telling her about how I had recently joined the paper and why it would be advantageous for local businesses to advertise.

She looked at me kindly and, much to my surprise, said yes and placed a quarter-page ad. I couldn't believe it! My first ad. I tried not to look so shocked and lose the sale. I was so grateful and I promised that in return I would bring friends into the restaurant whenever I could. Eventually, I came around with friends so often that she bought another ad and another ad. Soon, she had bought a year's worth of ads, and I, in turn, had brought nearly my entire residential college to York Street Noodle House. Its popularity spread. Business took off for both of us.

I next sold to Toad's Place, our local dance club, and soon thereafter secured the support of Yale agencies and establishments. When firms such as Goldman Sachs and McKinsey & Company came to recruit on campus, I would stop by their events and forge relationships, and they would later request to buy advertisements in *The Yale Herald*.

After one more semester, Jane retired, having reached term limits, and I was promoted. By the spring of junior year, I had become publisher of *The Yale Herald*. I immediately undertook measures to further cut costs by finding a lower-cost printer, reducing the use of color ink, surveying the campus to see where the newspaper was actually being read, and redistributing the newspaper toward those areas. These cost-cutting measures required a close collaboration with the editorial team, and the strengthened bond helped us to revitalize readership. As morale lifted, word spread across campus, and the size of the business team grew from two to ten to thirty. With more team members on board, I was able to divide us into different teams: Yale Agency Sales, Local Sales, and National Sales. And with a lot of hard work and an enterprising spirit, dollar by dollar, we brought the newspaper from near bankruptcy to record profitability. The team rejoiced.

DON'T WAIT FOR THE PERFECT OPPORTUNITY

I know firsthand your future depends on your willingness to say yes to opportunities even if they don't look perfect, and to go after what you want with everything you've got. Becoming the publisher of *The Yale Herald* was definitely a dream come true. But it didn't fall in my lap—nothing truly good ever does. I had to work for it and be willing to say yes to an opportunity that wasn't 100 percent perfect on paper, but was a chance for me to get involved and learn.

If I had seen the posting for financial analyst and pushed it aside because it wasn't exactly what I was looking for, I'd never have met Jane, stepped into that role, learned how to get beyond my natural shyness to sell, and ultimately found myself at the helm of a newspaper at twenty years old, in order to lead it from bankruptcy to profitability.

Very rarely will your dream job be listed on job boards. But if you know what your ideal job is, find another way into that organization or industry, excel at what you are doing, and you'll find yourself reaching your goal faster than you ever imagined.

This is yet another example of being flexible yet strategic.

Evaluating Opportunities

If you are having trouble determining whether an opportunity is right for you, take a moment to answer the following questions.

1. What skills could I learn from this job that I don't currently possess?
2. What people could this opportunity put me in contact with that might lead to something promising in the future?
3. What's the worst that could happen if I take on this role and it doesn't work out?

I had no idea those years working at *The Yale Herald* and bringing it back to profitability would be a key talking point on my resume after college, giving employers the confidence that I could have a more senior role in their organizations than they would typically have given to a recent college graduate. Yet it was an accelerator that demonstrated to them I was ready to roll up my sleeves—just as much as my formal college internships at Electronic Data Systems and Goldman Sachs. Despite the fact that I was young, my role at *The Yale Herald* proved that I had already taken the reins of something and steered it in the right direction.

Your path will obviously look different than mine, as will your goal, but know that with the right people inspiring you, and a willingness to look for opportunities at every turn, you, too, will be able to home in on your passions and realize your dream.

#YouAreAMogul

Follow in the footsteps set by someone you admire, and keep your eyes peeled for the many opportunities that could be accelerators. Learn to say yes, even if the job doesn't look perfect. It's the specific experiences and opportunities that you create for yourself that will become your calling card.

#IAmAMogul

By Dr. Jen Welter, the first female NFL coach

I never set out to make history. I never set out to be the "first" anything. My only goal was to pursue my love of sport, and that sport happened to be football. But growing up, I wasn't allowed to play because I was a girl. When I got to college, I started playing rugby, which was as close as I was going to get, and then I started playing flag football, and eventually found the women's league after college. It was such an incredible feeling to get to take the field for the first time, as a woman, and play the sport that I loved.

I didn't set any limits on where football could take me. I loved it; the competition, the camaraderie, the challenge of a group coming together to achieve a single goal. I pursued this passion of mine despite the fact that I was the only girl. Football was what I loved, and I pushed myself to be the best, and a part of this experience in any way I could. After I finished my doctorate in psychology, I wondered what it would be like to bring the knowledge that I had acquired, and a woman's perspective, onto the coaching staff of a team. It had never been done before. That didn't mean that it wasn't time for it to be done.

What's important about my journey is not the fact that I was the first to infiltrate the "boys' club" that was the NFL. **It's about knowing that your opportunities as young women are not narrowed because of your gender.** And if anyone tells you different, I have already proved that they are wrong.

We need to remove the ceiling society has set in place and know that we have the capacity to do anything we put our minds to. If there aren't any opportunities out there in the field that you love because of your gender, make those opportunities yourself.

I enjoy sports, and I of course love football. But I am no different from any of you reading this who have passions of your own. I've simply removed any barrier trying to prevent me from taking the next step. And my journey hasn't stopped yet. Yours hasn't either.

② VALUE YOUR VOICE

No matter what you hope to accomplish with your life, whether you want to create your own company, rise to the ranks of CEO, solve a problem in the world that is begging for a solution, or just live a life of purpose and meaning, to get there, you've got to learn to speak up. You've got to recognize the power of your voice, the value of your ideas, and that your perspective is urgently needed.

Yes, you may face stereotypes or biases, but only by developing confidence in who you are will you be able to break these down. Commit to valuing who you are and remaining authentically yourself across all aspects of life.

The fact is, whether you find yourself in the classroom, the conference room, or the boardroom, you may often look different, think differently, and talk differently than those around you, but that doesn't mean your voice isn't valid or essential to the conversation. You bring something important to the table. Your perspective is invaluable. And the more that you rise up and demand a seat at the table, the more diverse that table will be so that hopefully, one day, it will not be notable whether there is a male leader, female leader, or minority leader at the head of the table. There will just be a leader: you.

WEIGH NEXT STEPS CAREFULLY

I had always planned on going to business school as part of my path to creating my own company, but struggled with when would be the right time to attend. I remember all too well, as graduation from Yale drew nearer, I began to increasingly question what would be the right next step in this journey?

I wrote down this existential question as I prepared the speech I had been asked by classmates and professors to deliver at Yale graduation, in front of ten thousand. I know. Me, the shy girl. I was honored by the vote of confidence, but also sincerely hoped I wouldn't stutter onstage.

In the speech, I tried to channel our class's collective optimism but uncertainty. I quoted lyrics from Bon Jovi's "Livin' on a Prayer" (the song that famously closed out Toad's Place each night, and which a choir joined me onstage to sing during the speech, surprising and delighting the audience). I knew what I wanted to do in the long term, but was only "halfway there." Where should I go from here?

By the end of senior year, I had received a full-time offer from Credit Suisse, for a two-year analyst program in Mergers and Acquisitions where I would be able to hone my financial skill sets. I hoped to focus on companies within the technology and media sector, so that I would be able to learn to read their financial statements and understand their business models from a strategic level. Given my eventual goal to start my own technology and media company, this seemed in line.

But I also kept wondering about business school.

At my father's encouragement, I began to study for the GMAT during spring break. I had just seven days to prepare before the test date, and I grew increasingly nervous as the days passed quickly by. I had been scoring low on practice test after practice test. The night before the GMAT, I tossed back and forth in bed all night. But thankfully, when test time came, I realized that the practice tests were actually many times more difficult than the actual GMAT. The adrenaline and focus kicked in, and when my score arrived, it was high enough that I applied to my first choice: Harvard Business School.

It was during our senior class trip to Myrtle Beach, just days prior to graduation, that I got the notification. While a dozen friends from our graduating class were sleeping strewn about the floor of our hotel room, casualties of a late night out, my close friend Susannah pulled up next to me excitedly. I clicked on the email: I had been admitted to Harvard Business School.

I called my father and mother to tell them the unbelievable news. They cried tears of joy and pride, thrilled that I had this opportunity at age twenty-one. But there was a part of me that knew I needed more time and experience before attending. My gut was telling me that as much as I wanted to go to HBS, there would be a time for it. And that time was not right now.

I wondered if HBS would allow me to defer for two years so that I could work at Credit Suisse in the interim. I didn't want to turn down the spot at HBS, but I knew that the opportunity to learn more about finance would be invaluable. Fortuitously, HBS agreed to a deferment, and the next four years of my life were subsequently planned out for me.

It was fortunate that I paid attention to my instincts. By waiting two years, I was still one of the youngest in my class, but now I had some real-world work experience under my belt. My two years working at Credit Suisse in New York City flew by, filled with overseas trips, late-night dinners, financial models, and more PowerPoint presentations than I could count. I had met some great people, really sharpened my financial skills, and knew that New York City was a place where I wanted to live again. But I was so excited for this next part of my journey.

Soon enough, I found myself, suitcases in hand, settling onto the Harvard Business School campus and moving into One Western Avenue, apartment #621. I was now twenty-three years old. While I had certainly learned a lot working in the world of finance, I still arrived with the naïveté and wide-eyed enthusiasm of Elle Woods in *Legally Blonde*, minus the pink wardrobe.

DON'T LET AGE HOLD YOU BACK

My decision to go to business school was a key part of my journey that gave me the confidence to speak up in a room full of people unlike me, to find my voice, and to figure out how to stay authentically true to myself even when I looked and acted different than most of the people in my industry. It was a time of growth, discovery, and confidence building that I know accelerated my growth as a leader and future entrepreneur.

But you should know that going to business school is not essential to becoming a mogul. You can certainly have a successful career without an MBA. However, I do encourage any woman who so desires to pursue a business degree. It is, after all, one more way that we can work to establish parity in the workplace. Experts say that more women getting MBAs is key to both closing the CEO gender disparity and addressing persistent systemic issues—most important, the gender pay gap. The statistics are so well known that I probably don't need to quote them, but I will do so anyway because they are worth emphasizing: Caucasian women earn 80 percent on the dollar compared with Caucasian men for doing the same job. And for women of color, the statistics are even more dire: 63 percent on the dollar for African-American women, and 54 percent on the dollar for Hispanic women. Over the course of your career, that can add up to half a million dollars or more. Or, as I recently saw in a *Washington Post* article, by the end of October, if you are a Caucasian woman, you are pretty much working for free for the rest of the year. If you are a woman of color, that date starts in July or August.

Terrible, right?

This is an issue we care deeply about at Mogul. And why we strive every day to destroy the inequalities that led researchers to project when parity will be reached in the United States, if we continue at the current, incredibly slow rate of change: 2059 for Caucasian women, 2124 for African-American women, and 2233 for Hispanic women, according to the Institute for Women's Policy Research.

Harvard Business School was a place where I was confronted with these realities head-on. There was no way around it: the majority of my classmates were Caucasian men, much older than me. At HBS, they divide each class of nine hundred into ten sections of ninety people each. These are the people you take your classes with, who make up your study groups, and with whom you have dedicated social outings. I was placed in Section J, or what a few whispers around campus came to call "the Married Section." The average age of our class was about twenty-seven, but my specific section was composed of some of the most experienced in our class, people who had spent up to a decade in various industries, with families at home. This degree would enable them to reach the C-suite at their companies once they graduated.

I immediately felt like an outsider. Not just an outsider, but also an imposter. What did I have to contribute to conversation? What did I know about running a business? I frequently felt like I had nothing to say.

But I soon learned that I could allow my age to limit me, or I could nonetheless bring my perspective and remember that it, too, had value. Age, after all, is just a number; we all have had experience in living that allows us to form insights about businesses, business models, marketing strategies, and consumers. Whether you are the oldest in the room, or the youngest in the room, age doesn't matter. You have to try to find a way to feel confident in yourself. You may have experienced more in your twenty-five years on earth than someone who is fifty, just because of the opportunities you weren't afraid to go after. And you can be fifty and be just as innovative and creative as someone just out of college, if not more.

This is something I've faced my entire life. But don't let anyone look down on you because you are younger or older. It's natural to feel undermined when you are referred to as "too young" or "green." But take the opportunity to prove them wrong (and yourself right) by continuing to speak up, sharing your voice and perspective. I would not be where I am today if I had allowed other people's assumptions about my experience, knowledge, and drive to slow me down. My willingness to go after opportunities despite my young age was most definitely an accelerator for me. I was always ready to take advantage of an opportunity, even when I wasn't necessarily the most qualified candidate.

Address the Elephant in the Room with Humor

When I was generally the youngest person in the room and knew that age bias might work against me, I figured out a way to handle it when someone would ask my age. I would say: "I'm forty" with a smile, and they would laugh, because I did not look forty; if anything, I still looked eighteen. Then, I would follow it up with a joke, "You just can't tell because I'm Asian!" Now I had put to bed two things that might have been elephants in the room, my age and my race. Let me tell you, people left me alone after that. Gloria Steinem once said, "The truth will set you free, but first it will piss you off." Once I faced the truth of my situation head-on, I was set free and used humor to defuse a challenging situation. Humor is a great defuser. Let them realize through your humor how irrelevant it is for them to even ask your age.

SPEAK UP

The truth is, I didn't have time to be shy and hold back at Harvard. I had to learn how to speak up, and I had to learn fast, because at HBS, up to 50 percent of your grade can depend on class participation. HBS is based on the case-study method, where students read about a real-life business example (aka case study), and then the professor calls on students who have raised their hands to further discuss the predicament outlined in the case, in order to arrive at a collective conclusion. The case typically starts with a cold call, where the professor selects any student at "random." You never know what the question is going to be, or whom the professor is going to call on. You have to be prepared to answer, no matter what. And just my luck, I was often the cold call.

As I said, most of my classmates were men in their late twenties to midthirties who had spent half a decade to a decade working in consulting or private equity. With years of experience speaking up in meetings with clients or partners, speaking up in class at HBS was a breeze for them. They were confident and well-spoken, not shy about voicing their opinions. It sometimes seemed like they'd hardly even read the case study, but that didn't prevent them from sharing their impromptu thoughts anyway, spouting out their theories of what went wrong and what they would do to turn things around.

Meanwhile, I dreaded the moment when the professor might call my name. I would have read every single word of the case, but I wasn't as experienced in sharing my opinions, and responding to follow-up questions. I found myself shrinking in my chair, in hopes that the professor wouldn't see me. My natural shyness came back in full force.

I'm by nature a doer, not a talker. I prefer to prove my value through actions, not words. But there are times when you *have* to speak up and speak confidently. HBS was going to be a place where I had to learn to find my voice. I didn't like it at first. I wished that I could just be judged on projects and test scores, like before. I struggled with this new way of having to prove myself. But I know now that it was the most important lesson I learned at Harvard, and it has served me every single day in the years since I graduated.

Learning how to get people to value what you bring to the discussion is essential, whether you plan to launch your own business, are applying for a job, or have dreams of being a TED Talk superstar. You have to learn to be an effective communicator to succeed. It may not come naturally. That's okay. There are ways you can develop this skill set, just like any other. You may never love having to speak in front of others, but commit to becoming proficient at it, and not letting the fear keep you from pursuing opportunities that could be accelerators for your career.

I soon developed a strategy where I could feel confident and ready to share my thoughts if the professor were to call on me. I continued to do the work of reading the case thoroughly. That wasn't the issue. It was dealing with the semi-stage fright that would emerge when my name was called. I had to confront that empty space, that silence with all eyes on me, and be prepared to speak up.

So the night before class, after studying the case study inside and out, I would write down on a notecard the three main points that I took away from the case. I would write them down, word-for-word. Then, I would have talking points ready that I could potentially say in class the next day, in case I was subject to the cold call.

It felt good to be prepared. To know that if I was called on, I knew exactly what to say. The next time the professor called on me and I had my three points ready, I spoke up clearly and confidently. I even took a pause, in order to give the illusion that I didn't have every single word already written out. But it soon got to the point that if the professor didn't call on me, considering all the time I'd spent preparing, I would push myself to raise my hand to offer my points to the discussion. I was hyper-prepared; I knew that whatever I had to say would add to the discussion.

That gave me enough confidence to raise my hand and provide insights in each class.

Step-by-step, I was able to overcome my fear of speaking up, and my concern that I didn't have anything to offer to the discussion. I had developed a skill that would serve me incredibly well in the years to come: the ability to present on my feet and be able to showcase whatever opinion or perspective I had with supporting evidence or rationale. And to know without a doubt that my voice was valid.

Secrets to Speaking in Front of Others with Confidence

In the past year alone, I was asked to speak about Mogul over two hundred times. What was once my biggest nightmare, however, has become a pleasant part of my every day. To overcome my fear of public speaking, I developed key steps to help boost my confidence when sharing my voice. If this is a challenge you face as well, follow these key steps to master speaking in front of others:

1. Write down the central ideas or thoughts that you wish to share. If you're particularly new at public speaking, you may need to write these ideas out word-for-word like I used to. Practice reciting them over and over, until the words roll off your tongue. Then, for the meeting or speech, simply write down several key words that remind you of each main idea, in order to jog your memory, worrying less about the exact words to use and more about the message you're trying to communicate.

2. Focus on looking the audience in the eye, instead of staying focused on your notes. I would locate one person (someone

kind-looking or smiling) in each part of the room, with whom I would subsequently make regular eye contact. This would in turn make me more at ease.

3. Take your time speaking, pausing as necessary. I had a tendency to speak quickly during cold calls initially, in a rush to get over the pain. I realized that enunciating and speaking with intent made me appear more certain of what I had to say, and thus made the audience feel more certain of what I had to say, too.

4. Learn to add gestures that match your words. I would count off with my fingers if I was making points "1," "2," and "3," which added energy and displayed further confidence.

If you are unsure of whether you are coming across clearly, practice your talking points before your presentation, class, or board meeting. You can even videotape yourself on your phone and identify where there are places where you aren't speaking loudly enough, or don't talk with enough conviction. Speaking in front of people is a skill that must be practiced. It very rarely comes naturally, but is something that people work at, and dedicate time to perfecting. But just remember that the more you do it, the easier it gets. I am living proof of that.

BREAK DOWN BOUNDARIES

Unfortunately, we as women aren't often taught how to speak up, or that we should. Or we've internalized messages that in order to succeed in a male-dominated workplace, we must emulate men and erase all evidence of femininity; that we can't be our true selves. This leads us to shy away from positions of influence and impact. In the absence of females in leadership positions, we face a gendered socialization that teaches that politics and positions of leadership are reserved for men. For example, despite making up more than half of the population, in the U.S. House of Representatives women occupy just 19 percent of the 435 seats. In the Senate, the number is 21 percent. Women fill just 23.7 percent of statewide elected executive offices. And in the private sector, of the five hundred companies on the 2016 Fortune 500 list, only 21—a mere 4 percent—are headed by women.

As Marian Wright Edelman famously said, "You can't be what you can't see." Marian Wright Edelman was a young African-American girl growing up in the South in the 1950s. "All the external message of the South told me that I wasn't worth much," she said. "But I didn't believe it because my mother and father always made me believe that I could be anything." She took that belief to heart and went on to become the first African-American woman to pass the Mississippi Bar in 1961. As she watched poverty continue to devastate the South, even after the Civil Rights Act of 1964, she created the Children's Defense Fund, the first lobby devoted to children. In fact, the Children's Defense Fund is where one of the first female U.S. presidential candidates went to work after law school. Perhaps the seeds that she could be the first female president were born from Hillary Clinton watching a woman as determined to break down barriers as Marian Wright Edelman.

We need more women in leadership positions to show young girls that they can be leaders; they *should* be leaders; that they were *born to be* leaders.

But even when we make inroads, women leaders are less likely to be celebrated. Nancy Pelosi became the first female speaker of the house in 2007, but was not featured on the cover of any national news magazine for her entire four-year run. John Boehner, when he was elected to that position in 2010, was on the cover of five in his first two weeks.

Since the 2016 U.S. presidential election results, we have begun to see an uprising of women willing to run for office across the States. We have realized that we have to be the ones breaking down boundaries and demolishing the stereotypes. Condoleezza Rice once said: "You can't wait for role models to look like you. If Sally Ride, the first female astronaut, had been waiting for a female astronaut role model, she would have never done it!"

Just because it hasn't happened yet doesn't mean it's impossible. We have to ignore the years of socialization that say that women can only be certain things. We created Mogul to be a place where you know that your voice is worthy, and that we want to hear from you. Any user can post material because we wanted women to enter the discussion, not be passive observers but realize they can contribute themselves. Being a user of the platform allows you to realize that you have a voice that the world needs, that what you have to say matters. **The more you value your voice, the more you will realize how much you have to offer the world, the more you will be willing to pursue leadership positions and not worry about feeling out of place.** And when you come across a barrier that does try to limit you, diminish you, or belittle you, you'll know that together our voices can demolish it.

BATTLING UNCONSCIOUS BIAS

But sometimes, even though *you* know your voice is valid, there are variables in effect that limit your success. At HBS, the top 5 percent of the class earns a distinction called the Baker Scholar, an honor that was known to open numerous doors. But in 2009, a year before I entered, just 14 percent of Baker Scholars were women, despite the fact that they made up almost 40 percent of the class. No one could understand why this was happening. It wasn't that Harvard was admitting lesser candidates to bulk up the number of women. Women were admitted with the same test scores and levels of experience as men.

Given that 50 percent of your grade at HBS consists of your class participation grade, the administration began to wonder if it was due to the fact that women weren't speaking up in class. At the time, professors were trusted to recall accurately who spoke in class, noting in their grade books after each session the students who had contributed to the discussion. Most professors at Harvard Business School are male. Just 20 percent of the tenured faculty is female. Could there be a gender bias involved in recalling which students truly spoke up in class?

In 2013, a year after I graduated, when the majority of Baker Scholars continued to be male, HBS decided to add stenographers to the classrooms so professors would no longer rely on possibly biased memories of who said what.

And with that simple addition, it became clear: it wasn't that women weren't speaking up. It was that the professors were more likely to remember the men. Women were receiving lower grades because of the unconscious bias of their professors.

After the addition of stenographers in the classroom, the percentage of Baker Scholars who were women increased from just 11 percent in 2009 to 38 percent in 2013, a number that closely mirrored their representation in the overall class.

It is impossible for us to determine how this kind of gender bias affects women across the board, not just in schools and universities, but when they are considered for promotions and job opportunities. I wish I had an easy solution to help you deal with other people's biases. The fact is, we can't control what other people remember. But we can do our part to address the issue by helping people to become more aware of how we are each unconsciously biased and how this is reflected in our day-to-day actions; and then work to overcome those biases.

That is an important part of Mogul's mission. By developing

trainings in collaboration with business leaders and experts on unconscious bias as well as inclusive leadership, Mogul has become a leader in ensuring gender equity in the workplace. It trains hundreds of thousands of business leaders across Fortune 1000 companies and more, on what biases they may personally exhibit as they review a resume, conduct an interview, or assess promotions, for example. Companies want, just like Harvard Business School, to do better and be better. They just weren't equipped with how to do it. Until now.

REMAIN YOUR AUTHENTIC SELF

I know that we won't be able to solve these problems overnight. But my hope, in creating Mogul, was to address many of them. To show you that you can become a mogul, and that you can pursue success and significance just as much as anyone around you. And do so by remaining your authentic self.

At HBS, my classmates and I often discussed this spectrum of female stereotypes: on one hand, if you were too warm and kind, you were likely to be viewed as incompetent; on the other hand, if you were cold and unemotional, you were likely to be viewed as mean but competent. It was a lose-lose situation. Why did this have to be the case? I opted just to be myself. But I continued to wonder about this as I saw some of my classmates begin to prioritize coldness over kindness in order to be taken seriously, erasing all emotionality.

I might have eventually bought into that mind-set as well. But then I met Stephanie, another woman in my section who wasn't about to change who she was just because of what others thought of her. Stephanie was also not your typical HBS student. An engineering major from Purdue, she looked just like Reese Witherspoon, with long blond hair, a megawatt smile, and a white miniature dog named Tofu. She, like me, stuck out like a sore thumb in our section; we were both not yet married and known to be sweet, and I could tell that she didn't want to have to change who she was to succeed in business, either. During our first week of class, we both offered to help organize the food for our section retreat in the fall. A few hours shopping for ninety people at Costco, combined with our subsequent road trip to Vermont, where we were to set up the food before everyone else arrived, cemented a best friendship and everlasting bond that has seen us support each other through thick and thin—from the classroom, to the workplace, through every relationship and more. Stephanie has gone on to become one of the most successful female executives in the health-care industry. And just like with Diane, my friend from high school, I was a bridesmaid in Stephanie's wedding years later. We still text each other "good morning" every day.

During January of that first year, I went on an HBS trip to Vietnam, where students would have the opportunity to assist various companies in need of business insights. There I met Maya, another business school classmate, who was Lebanese and Greek. Maya graduated in the top 0.5 percent of her class at the American University in Beirut, and was gorgeous and an international jetsetter, quite parallel to the otherwise incomparable Amal Clooney. But most endearingly, Maya was also genuine, frank, and direct; she told it like it was, though she also coupled her remarks with humor, wit, and a charming French accent, disarming her audience and immediately establishing a rapport with them. Seeing her stick to being 100 percent authentically true to herself was incredibly refreshing and empowering. Still to this day, whenever I have a tough question that requires a tough answer, I will message or call Maya wherever she may be in the world. She will always tell it to me straight, usually while on a plane to whichever city she is headed next.

If Stephanie and Maya hadn't been by my side—two other women who weren't afraid to be smart, feminine, kind, and authentically themselves—I might have developed a harder shell and more closely followed the mold set before us. But with each other's encouragement, we strived to not bend to the pressure around us to look or act a certain way. **When you help another woman succeed, all women succeed. We are so much stronger as allies, and we need each other to move ahead.**

I've endeavored to remain my authentic self throughout my professional life, so that we can try to change the perception. We don't have to be cold and unemotional to be taken seriously as women in business. In fact, strong feminine leadership is highly coveted given its remarkable results. Need an example? Tech startups that have a female executive average a 35 percent higher return on investment. **It is our opportunity to stand together and demonstrate the value of our diverse perspectives, not by acting more masculine, but by continuing to be our kind, competent, authentic selves, for which we should never feel regret.**

It's true; times were different not even that long ago. One of my friends told me that it wasn't until she had reached the C-suite of a Fortune 100 company that she felt she could really be herself at work. She had worried that she wouldn't receive the respect that would be necessary for the next promotion. So, role after role and decade after decade, she had put on a more masculine attitude, in order to fit the mold that was expected to achieve success in the workplace. Yet as soon as she was promoted to the C-suite, she began to wear more comfortable clothes around the office. She became sweeter, kinder. She became herself.

But today, things are beginning to change, and it's up to us to continue that momentum. Being a great leader doesn't mean you have to mimic masculine habits. Having a strong feminine leadership style can lead to the best results. You can lead with compassion and care and get the same or even better results than if you were strict, nonemotional, and demanding. It is up to us to redefine these words and these stereotypes. We've done it with the word "mogul." Why not redefine what it means to be a leader? What if a leader didn't mean someone who looked down from above, shouting dictates and orders, but meant someone who came alongside, supported, uplifted, and encouraged? Once we see more women in leadership positions empowered to be feminine in their leadership style, we will no longer feel like we have to adopt masculine traits to be considered a leader.

Even so, at any given moment, you may feel this tension between being who you are and being who you feel the world needs you to be. But it is always better to choose the former. By remaining your authentic self, you'll experience an ease of life. You won't need to expend energy maintaining a mask—a mask that was born out of peer pressure, or a desire to not stand out. You were meant to stand out. You were meant to have your unique ideas and thoughts and perspectives. You were meant to have the kind of confidence that can only come from being your true and natural self. You were meant to be you.

Cultivating Confidence

It took me many years and countless times where I kept my mouth shut before I consistently raised my hand, offered my opinion, and stepped into the discussion. If you are feeling like you are the one person who is "different" in the room, take a moment to recognize that that shouldn't hold you back but instead encourage you to speak up. This, like everything else, takes practice.

If you are facing an industry event, a board meeting, or an interview where you know you will be facing a roomful of people unlike you, acknowledge what an important thing you are doing. You are taking one more step for each of us to claim our place at the table. You are saying there is room here for me, too. Take a moment, and remember who you are. Where you come from. The perspective that you bring. Play an individual highlight reel of your accomplishments to boost your confidence.

Then repeat the following mantras.

I will not let other people's stereotypes limit where I can go.
We need diverse people and perspectives in the conversation.
My perspective is important.
I deserve to be here.

COMMUNICATE CONSTANTLY, CONSISTENTLY, AND CLEARLY

So far, I've focused here on my growth as a person during business school because I do think that facing some of these stereotypes, biases, and conditionings was more important than any one lesson I could learn in the classroom. That said, I did learn a lot in the classroom, too, and the lessons I remember most significantly focused on one key theme: communication.

One of the most important ideas I got from business school that I use to this day is the concept of Repetition, Repetition, Repetition! I heard this in a class taught by Professor Robert Kaplan. When expressing something to your team members, the first time you say something, they hear you; the next time you say it, they get it; and by the following time you repeat it, they really absorb it. You cannot state your objective just once and hope that someone will so quickly capture all that you intended; you must repeat and repeat to make sure it is understood and never forgotten. I have used that lesson many times in my career and as I've built Mogul.

Another key lesson that I valued greatly is the concept of goal alignment. If you want your employees to be fulfilled and strive to work even harder, you have to make sure they understand the big-picture thinking of the company and that their goals align with the goals of the company. This was what my friends and I most often noted was missing from our work at our respective employers, particularly at the junior level. We frequently saw little connection with how our presentations and number-crunching were impacting the goals of the institution as a whole. As a result, work could sometimes become tedious and unfulfilling. If the leaders of the companies we had been at had brought us junior team members more into the fold by communicating how our work was contributing to the whole, we would have been much more satisfied, and more likely to pour ourselves into our work. In the end, it all comes down to communication. You have to communicate with each other to create full buy-in. Let everyone know what you are working toward. The best way to do this is to develop goals together, so that the goals aren't coming only from the top down, but are also coming from the ground up. Observe where these top-down and bottom-up goals align and misalign, and communicate and compromise on those points. Being a part of goal-setting creates more buy-in and commitment from your team members. It allows a feeling of camaraderie and shared interest that makes the workplace much more fulfilling for all involved.

Communication is also essential if you are cofounding a business with someone. You want to ensure that you are communicating with each other about your individual goals for the company. In business school, during a class on the Founder's Dilemmas with Professor Noam Wasserman, we discussed the challenge that many entrepreneurs face: Do they want to be "rich," or do they want to be "king"? If your motive is to be rich, then you will make choices that enable your company to grow as quickly as possible, even if it means giving up some control. If your cofounder, on the other hand, is focused on being and staying king, they prioritize control over cash. They may want to turn down certain opportunities that could lead to explosive growth if it means sacrificing some control of their kingdom. If these goals are not explicitly communicated ahead of founding a company, two cofounders are bound to find themselves facing serious conflict. It remains the reason why 65 percent of startups fail today.

Today, I frequently look back upon my time at HBS, to recall these lessons and apply them at Mogul. But more so, I remember how much I grew, how much confidence I gained, and how helpful it was to recognize that my voice was necessary, valuable, and important, so that I was able to share it in every job I had going forward.

#YouAreAMogul

You don't need to get a fancy degree in order to have something to add to the conversation. You have a voice that matters and that the world urgently needs. Value your voice, share it often, and step into positions of impact and influence wherever you can. It won't be handed to you; you have to reach for it.

BEN HASSETT

#IAmAMogul

**By Nina García, editor in chief of *ELLE*
magazine and judge on *Project Runway***

I grew up in South America and came to America when I was fifteen. I was never going to fit in working in the American fashion industry. My frame of reference for beauty, and what a woman should be, was shaped by the Colombian culture. But it was that unique background, that ability to see things differently, that helped me rise to where I am today.

The fact that I was an immigrant working in America's fashion world gave me a unique point of view. I saw fashion with a different eye, and I always considered that a plus. I truly *believed* it was a benefit, so in turn, it became beneficial. You have to have that confidence that your voice is valid. I knew I was bringing something different to the table than everyone else, and that distinct perspective that I wasn't afraid to share is what led to my success in the industry.

The role of an editor, and that of a creative director, is to give the magazine a point of view, a voice, and a perspective that is all its own. We could not just hope to emulate others. That would have caused us to get lost in a very crowded industry. It is no different for you. **You must access your authentic perspective in order to make inroads in whatever industry you want to go into. People need to hear your voice that is different from theirs. You have to be yourself.**

If you think about fashion, and the most inspiring designers, they succeed because they are putting their point of view out into the world in a way that others haven't before. That is the only way to make a name for yourself in fashion. See things differently and dare to put it out there. Fashion, by its very nature, empowers you to express your individuality. That's why I've always said, you don't need to follow the trends, you can make the trends!

Whether you are in an industry like fashion that is dominated by females, or an industry like banking that tends to be dominated by males, have the confidence to be authentically yourself, develop your own personal voice and style, and it will allow you to truly stand out from the crowd.

③ CRUSH IT IN CORPORATE LIFE

Some people are convinced that the path to success is about single-minded determination: you see a goal and you hammer away at it until you achieve it. That wasn't my path, and it hasn't been the path of most of the women in the Mogul community. This is, in part, because old career models are fading away. The corporate ladder that was once a straight path up is now old and rusty.

It's an exhilarating thought: most of us won't spend our careers at one company, climbing one corporate ladder. We don't have an eye on the corner office because there are no more corner offices—doors are opening and walls are coming down, literally and figuratively. In fact, recent studies have shown that only 13 percent of millennials aspire to be the CEO or president of an existing company. By contrast, nearly 70 percent of millennials hope to start their own business someday.

I love the ambition of this generation. But the key word is "someday." Very few of us will start a company right after college. Most of us will still spend years of our lives working for other people. And that is a wonderful opportunity. Despite the fact that I always knew I wanted to create my own company, I also knew I had a lot to learn before I was ready to do so. Therefore, I always approached every job I took on as an opportunity to learn a skill set that would help me down the road.

Too often, we look for opportunities that will enhance our resumes, instead of staying focused on *what could I learn here?* And *will this be an opportunity to experience something new?*

Even if you are not yet working in your dream job, don't wish these years away! Consider this time in your life your training. This is your chance to learn from the greats. To soak up knowledge and strategies and build up your skill sets while you further refine your passions that will help you determine where your career will go. Olympians don't automatically find themselves winning gold medals. They spend years getting ready to attain greatness, training with the best, developing their skills, so that when they step out into the arena, they win the gold.

DEVELOP YOUR SKILLS

Not all jobs are equal training grounds, however. So I advise you to think carefully about what jobs you take on. I understand, we all need a paycheck, and sometimes any job is better than no job. But I've always thought first and foremost about how the job offered would provide the skill sets to help me run a media and technology company one day. What skills would it develop in me that could be useful in my career down the road? I felt that to be a business owner, I needed to know every facet of the industry I would be in, inside and out. I needed to be a kind of jack-of-all-trades. Though you might like to just imagine being the leader, getting to call all the shots and make all the decisions, the truth is, to build a company, you've got to initially have your hand in all aspects of the company. Finance. Operations. Content. Marketing. Distribution. Strategy. Business development. Branding. Product. Technology.

These skill sets became a kind of checklist for me very early on, and I weighed every opportunity that came my way with whether or not it would help me develop in one of these areas.

Perhaps you find yourself in a position where you've never allowed yourself to go after what you truly want. Paying bills and paying off student loans have taken priority. And that is okay. But I know that the business world today is an incredibly creative place, and there are so many ways you can make an impact in the world. So if you find yourself in a job that does not light you up with passion and joy, I invite you to begin to dream. What is your ideal job? And what are the steps you might take to get there? It may seem like there are a million steps between where you are today and where you want to go, but I hope you have seen by now that there are always accelerators that can get you there much faster. **So dream big. And then make choices that will allow you to develop the skill sets to get you there one day.** You don't have to know the exact way; you may just have a general idea or direction. And you aren't going to get there immediately. But learn to approach your current situation strategically and acquire as many valuable, transferable skills as you can. These days working for other people should not be wasted. They are golden opportunities.

If you don't know your end goal, don't worry. These years can also be a great opportunity to try out different industries and determine your strengths, weaknesses, passions, and, ultimately, what you want to pursue.

Determining Your End Goal and What Skills to Develop

Take a moment to think about what industry you want to be in and what you want to be doing five years from now. Then think backward about what you need to learn and know to achieve that goal. Think of specific, transferable skills. Then create a checklist, as I did with my checklist of skills, so that you don't get sidetracked along the way.

If you don't know what you want to ideally be doing, use the following questions to help get your creative juices flowing and begin to realize where your passions, strengths, and interests lie.

What am I naturally good at?

What do I truly love doing?

What do I really want?

What do I really, really want?

What is the deeper urge behind that goal?

Answering these questions will not only help you determine what you love to do and should therefore do, but get to the root of the kind of impact you truly desire to have on the world.

STAY FOCUSED ON THE END GOAL

It is not like there weren't times when I, too, questioned whether I was doing the right thing or in the right job. While I learned a lot in finance during those years before business school, the part of me that wanted to make a difference, that wanted my family to be proud of me, was fighting with my current situation, which was spending my days crunching numbers. I just couldn't see the impact I was making and felt discouraged. In fact, though I had just one more year before HBS was to start, I struggled with whether I was on the right path, and applied for an unpaid internship at the United Nations. Yet, it wasn't applicable to any of the skill sets I had wished to learn.

When the UN accepted my application, I called my father. I told him why I was thinking about leaving my current finance job for the UN, and how much I respected what the UN was doing. But I couldn't get around the fact that if I quit, I would barely have scratched the surface of what I needed to learn in finance for my end goal.

In a way, I think I called him that day because I wanted him to tell me I would be making a mistake. And sure enough, that's what he did.

"Tiffany," he said, "I know that you want to make a difference. And you will. But right now, you are putting in the hours to learn the skills necessary to make that difference. If you quit right now, you are going to look back and feel like you didn't have a chance to fully round out your knowledge of this area. If you are ever going to pursue starting something, put your heart into it and finish this out. Become the best you can be at it. Then move on to the next thing."

It was my own cherished philosophy, which I seemed to have forgotten.

He paused. "The reality is, Tiffany, that one day the UN will invite you, not as an unpaid intern, but as a guest because you will have created something of global impact."

My father reminded me of something important that day. Sometimes, we have to be patient with our goals. We have to be present in the moment, and not always try to fast-forward to where we want to go. I turned down the UN internship and finished my time in finance.

But not before communicating with my superiors at Credit Suisse about how I hoped to see more of the impact I was having so that I could further pour myself into the work. In turn, they granted me permission to fly to the cities where each of my Mergers and Acquisitions deals was scheduled to close—from West Palm Beach, Florida, to Jackson, Ohio, to Jena, Germany—so I could see for myself the impact each would have on the companies' teams, their management, and the surrounding communities. It helped me to put faces to the company names that I had stared at for so long, from my lone computer in New York. And from those trips,

I became friends with our clients and familiar with their products, and understood firsthand the impact that could transpire from being adept at finance. It enriched my overall experience, all of which was a great foundation for my subsequent years at business school.

By the time I graduated from HBS, I had an offer to work full-time at HBO within their Distribution and Marketing division, where I had interned the summer between business school years. But I was ready to expand my skill sets further. My finance skill set was on point. I could check that off the list. I had developed significant insight on distribution. I could also check that off the list. I therefore accepted a job offer from CBS, where I would help lead strategic initiatives and partnerships for the organization's growth, learning extensively as well as building relationships across the intersection of TV, radio, web, and mobile. That would enable me to develop expertise in operations, strategy, and business development. All that remained were content, marketing, branding, product, and technology. Still a lot to tackle, but I would be well on my way to feeling competent and confident to start my own endeavor.

Tips for Accepting a Job Offer

When I first landed job offers early in my career, there weren't enough resources to turn to that would outline how to negotiate for the best salary or terms. Yet another reason for creating Mogul. However, I would always make sure to research industry benchmarks, so I knew what was standard in the field. And when I would receive a call from HR with an offer, I would say thank you, make it clear that I was excited about the company and about the team, and that I would consider and reconnect shortly. If I had another offer on the table, I would be sure to be transparent that I had received multiple offers, but I was especially excited for this company. Then I would call back a day later and ask for about a 10 to 20 percent higher salary as well as a higher role with greater responsibility. That might simply mean adding "senior" to the title and getting one or two more projects, but I've always viewed that as half a step closer to where you wanted to be.

Typically, if you ask, you will get more than what you were initially offered; and that was the case for me and CBS. If someone says no to your request, it doesn't mean you can't take the job. But you have asked for what you thought you were worth. And if the reasons for why they could not accommodate your request were non-budgetary, you can always begin the conversation of what you would need to accomplish in order to eventually get to that rate. This way, you accept the job knowing ahead of time what goals you and your company have set so that you can reach that role or salary in the near future.

Negotiating your salary is a key accelerator. Did you know that a 2016 Glassdoor study found that 68 percent of women did not negotiate their salary? That is money that you are leaving on the table. (Only 52 percent of men made that mistake.) Don't miss this opportunity. Go in with a goal, and if they aren't willing to match your request, figure out what your BATNA is, or best alternative to a negotiated agreement. In other words, know your answers to these questions: What is the minimum salary that you're willing to accept, and what are the implications if you don't ultimately take what is offered? Calmly reference your other options, without your counterpart feeling threatened. If your counterpart is receptive to your negotiation and unwilling to let you walk away, then you'll find yourself meeting somewhere in the middle, and you are still ahead of where you would have been if you had just accepted their first offer.

KILL IT BY OVER-DELIVERING

There is one skill that I believe will be an accelerator for you no matter what job you find yourself in. One maxim that I believe will guarantee success. One attitude that will carry you exactly where you want to go. I've used it for every single job I've taken on, and it has never failed me.

You've got to kill it and over-deliver on every task you are given.

And I mean every task. There is no task too small for you. In any job, you want to be focused on how you can be of service, in big ways and small. Early in your career or tenure at a company, your tasks may be as mundane as making coffee, scheduling appointments, or answering the phone. But those tasks can be performed impeccably well. Make the best cup of coffee you can, exactly how your manager likes it. Set up a scheduling system that never fails, that allows you or those you work for to know exactly where they need to be at all times. Answer the phone promptly and kindly and as if a *New York Times* reporter were watching you and going to write a front-page article about how you answered that phone. A friend of mine once told me that, while working for a political campaign, she learned she and her coworkers would have to manually send thousands of letters out, which would require them to staple thousands of papers together and lick thousands of stamps (this must have been before the introduction of self-adhesive stamps). The rest of her coworkers visibly groaned, whereas she rejoiced in the task and became so passionate about licking stamps for that three-day period that she became the best anyone had ever seen! By the end of the three days, she had been promoted (though with a very sore tongue, a small price to pay for making her way up the ranks).

You see, the key is not just doing those tasks well, but to go above and beyond what is asked of you. This mind-set truly helped me rise faster and take on more at CBS in my two years there than I ever could have imagined.

When I first joined CBS, I loved being back in New York. I moved into an apartment at Sixty-Ninth Street and Central Park West, and would walk to the CBS offices in Midtown through Central Park. No day was ever the same at CBS, and I relished the fast pace and the freedom the company gave me to set my own schedule and take on additional responsibilities. Because of the experience I had accumulated throughout my time at Yale and HBS as well as within finance and media, I was brought in at a high level and became one of the youngest directors. I was also given a lot of freedom in my job. It was very entrepreneurial, which I loved, and given my own hustler mentality, it meant that I was able to take on more and more.

CBS is an enormous entity with a large number of properties. They had TV stations, radio stations, both national and local, and at the time were trying to figure out how to distribute these properties digitally across web, mobile web, and mobile app, which were becoming new venues for people to watch content.

As director of business development, I was charged with developing and executing new initiatives for growth, such as revenue growth or user growth, which often meant developing strategic partnerships. I often came up with ideas that hadn't been presented before. I would propose to other media organizations that we partner on live events, in order to live stream their concerts and encourage sponsorship on our sites. Or if we had video content that wasn't being viewed, I would reach out to these organizations to see if they wanted our content across their channels, thereby increasing viewership for all. I loved being able to support startups, in particular; if I championed them internally, CBS would ultimately agree to partner. We would cut them a check, enabling these startups to grow further and faster, while we gained visibility and reach. A win for everyone. And when my superiors observed my ability to take on new projects, come up with creative solutions, and over-deliver, they kept giving me more and more responsibility.

Developing Your Hustler Mentality

As you read about my experiences, you'll see that I've always had a hustler mentality. A hustler mentality means you are a fighter who won't stop until you accomplish what you set out to; you are resourceful and willing to roll up your sleeves, without relying on someone else; and you are bold and courageous, able to overcome whatever obstacle in order to make that connection, close that deal, or make that opportunity a reality.

This mind-set is obviously imperative for entrepreneurs, but it also really serves you in any job. When you are a hustler, you become someone that people depend on because they have seen you, time and time again, give your all to every job you are given, and often, find unusual and unexpected solutions to problems. Hustlers don't expect to have everything handed to them on a silver platter, from a raise to a promotion to a fulfilling job. They are incredibly driven and showcase moxie, dedication, and commitment. So when you find yourself feeling burnt out in your career, think about how you could apply your hustler mentality to the work you've been given. Is there a way you could make your task more interesting, think about it in a different way, or suggest something creative to your manager?

DISCOVER YOUR DIFFERENTIATOR

During my tenure at CBS, I quickly developed a specialty in an area that comparatively few else within the industry had expertise in at the time: digital distribution. This was a new trend in the marketplace. For almost fifty years, content had been primarily distributed via radio, television, or print. But with the rise of not just the Internet, but soon thereafter streaming services and social media platforms, there were thousands of additional channels for distribution. Because of the insights I had gained while at HBO, developing distribution strategies for their new app HBO GO, and because there was no veteran at CBS dedicated to this continually evolving realm, it soon became my domain, despite my age and lack of tenure.

After just a year at CBS, I found myself overseeing the start of our digital distribution efforts. This accelerated my growth, giving me access to people and meetings I otherwise would not have been exposed to.

Find your differentiator, or a skill set that you develop that few others have. This allows you to rise quicker because you are the only one people can turn to. Being different is good; use it to your advantage.

Unfortunately, instead of finding a differentiator, all too often people follow others who have found wealth and prestige on one certain path. I saw this mentality at both Yale and HBS. There were certain paths that people tended to go down even if they would never lead to anything that resembled their true passion. For example, recruiters from companies with structured recruitment programs would always arrive on campus at Yale or HBS in the fall. Students would flock to these recruiters, who offered jobs that both were lucrative and came with a kind of pedigree and reputation people sought. Plus, it meant you had a job offer before Christmas. You'd have the rest of your final school year to relax, knowing your future.

At HBS, most graduates ended up taking jobs in the world of finance or consulting, the very two fields the majority of students had initially come from. I was one of the few business school graduates interested in working in media. But when you dare to do something different, it can become an accelerator.

My best friend from high school, Diane, shared this mentality. As mentioned previously, Diane was top of our class, one of the smartest girls I'd ever met. She wanted to become a doctor. But while she was at Harvard Medical School, obtaining her MD-PhD, she watched everyone determine their specialties, and noticed there were certain areas that people tended to flock to: dermatology and orthopedics, because they offered good pay and decent hours. Or surgery, because it brought with it an aura of prestige as well as high salaries.

Very few doctors specialized in pediatric neurology. But Diane knew that children with neurological conditions needed just as much help as any other sick person. So after graduating from HMS, she went into that field and is an absolute rock star in it. Now, she probably would have become a rock star in whatever field she chose, but because there were so few talented doctors pursuing this specialty, Diane was truly an anomaly and highly in demand. Choosing that specialty was an accelerator for her.

I'm not saying that you should only pursue specialties because no one else is doing them. I do suggest that you get creative about how you might apply your passion to a problem or industry in a new way. Don't get caught up in the rat race that says there is one path to success. Find what your differentiator can be, and then go after it with all your heart.

BECOME AN "INTRAPRENEUR"

An entrepreneur is always looking for new opportunities, new ways to approach a problem, new ways to create revenue no

matter where they are working. An "intrapreneur" is someone who takes the mind-set of an entrepreneur and applies it to the company that they work for. This is an extremely valuable skill set in any job. Don't be afraid to show this side of you in the workplace.

Every day that I was at CBS, I was always ready and willing to do more and take on more. I jumped at every chance to take on any additional responsibility and create new business opportunities for the assets I helped oversee to further grow and scale.

About a year and a half into my tenure, one of the presidents within the company approached me to collaborate with him more directly. I had received their annual "All-Star Award" for my work that past year, and he formally offered to further support my development if, in exchange, I would only spend 25 percent of my time on business development from that moment onward. The rest would be spent shadowing him directly, collaborating on thought leadership and participating in strategic meetings across departments so I could support his decision making, as well as creating presentations for his own meetings so I would learn how the company was run from the highest level.

This was a huge accelerator for me. During that time, I was invited into meetings that I wouldn't have had access to for several years had he not issued this invitation. Because I was in the majority of meetings he attended, I was able to see all the problems and issues that management must regularly address. I could watch firsthand how he handled those problems. I witnessed the pressure sales leaders were constantly under, assessed budget sheets, and essentially soaked up every part of the experience.

Most of the jobs he gave me were invigorating and exciting. Some of them were understandably more mundane. But I poured myself into each task wholeheartedly, always asking what I could learn from the task, and of course how I could go beyond what was asked of me. Over-delivering is not something one does to get started in one's career; it is something successful people do throughout their career.

Developing Your Entrepreneurial Mindset in the Workplace

These tips will inevitably impress those above you:

- When there is a new project being discussed or you see an opportunity forming where no one else is paying attention, speak up and offer to spearhead that initiative. Don't assume that someone more senior will see the opportunity or volunteer for the job. Always be the first to volunteer in meetings or for taking on new responsibilities.
- Pay attention to what your manager's highest priority is or what they feel is lacking, and then deliver a solution. They will recognize that you have your priorities right as well.
- Ask to attend meetings with the people to whom you report. They may say no, but if they say yes, you now have another opportunity to learn, and an additional opportunity to volunteer to help.
- When you are given a job description, go above and beyond. Do what is asked of you, but then think about what else might be helpful. If you have to do something more mundane, trick your mind into believing it is the most exciting thing you have ever had to do. Your positive attitude will make others excited to work with you.

ASK FOR WHAT YOU WANT (BECAUSE NO ONE ELSE WILL ASK FOR YOU)

Obviously promotions are essential to rising in the ranks. A promotion allows you to accelerate your stature in your industry of choice and often comes with a pay raise as well. But here is the thing. **If you don't ask, you don't get.** In a 2015 PayScale survey, 57 percent of people *don't ask for raises*, and women are less likely to ask for raises than men. So we have to learn to ask. But we can't just go in with a demand and expect to get what we want. It benefits you to have a strategy in place so that you are guaranteed a yes.

Here's what I learned to do. Six months into any job I had, I would meet with my supervisor and let them know that in the future, I would love to be considered for a promotion or a raise. And then I would ask them a targeted question: *What is your expectation for what I need to accomplish and what milestones do I need to hit, in order to receive a promotion?*

Encourage their answer to be as concrete as possible. What would they like to see from you in the next six months in order to warrant a promotion? When you get details, you can walk out of that room knowing exactly what you need to accomplish. Then, when you go back in for your one-year performance review, you've already hit those benchmarks or goals. It makes them much more likely to say yes to a promotion; you've hit the target already. How could they say no? Make it difficult for them to say no.

It may seem crazy to begin asking about such things just six months into a job. But I am a firm believer that you cannot just wait for a promotion to come to you. Your supervisors may be focused on their own careers and meeting their own goals. They may not be actively looking to make sure you accomplish yours. **You cannot leave promotions and raises to chance. You must be proactive about them. It's important to be in charge of your own destiny.** Having your future in your own hands is a position you should always strive to put yourself in. Why wait around for someone else's whim to kick in? Why not enhance your chances by communicating your aim and receiving someone's expectations? This in turn deepens and strengthens your working relationship, as they'll be rooting for you, while also helping you accomplish your goals quicker. It's all about communication and transparency.

This is so much bigger than asking for a raise or a promotion. Speaking up is a global issue that women face. When you don't ask for what you want, you don't give yourself the chance to receive it. If there is something that you wish for, voice it. Voice your hopes and opinions. Think of the women who stood up for their right to vote or right to drive in their respective countries, risking their lives to do so. It took years, and some arrests, and a lot of pain to accomplish their goal. But they are now finally getting the right to do so.

In the last chapter we talked about how to value your voice. Now it is time to use it to ask for what you want.

My years at CBS were a huge time of growth for me, a time of acquiring new skills and building friendships with those in the media industry. But it wasn't just my hours inside the office building that helped me understand the ins and outs of running a company. It was just as much the time I spent outside the office after hours that contributed to the company's launch. In the next chapter, we'll talk about the all-important side hustle.

Asking for a Promotion

Today is the day you set yourself up for promotion. Write down these three opening lines on a notecard as thought-starters (just as I used to do at HBS!):

- Thank you, [name], for taking the time to see me today. I would love to discuss with you my future at the company, and hear your thoughts. I love working here and working for you, and it would be wonderful to collaborate with you on my path ahead.
- What is your expectation for what I need to accomplish and

what milestones I need to hit overall, in order to receive a promotion?

- What would you specifically like to see from me in the next one month, three months, six months, in order to warrant a promotion six months from now?

Ask your manager if you can set a time today to talk. Then, walk in with confidence, close the door, and go for it. You can do this!

#YouAreAMogul

When you learn to give your all to every job you are given, big or small, you show the world how much you are capable of. Over-deliver and kill it in everything you do. This maxim will never lead you astray, and I guarantee you'll find yourself on the path to becoming a mogul.

DAVID BEYDA

#IAmAMogul

By Ann Misiaszek Sarnoff, president of BBC Worldwide Americas, and member of the Board of Directors at PayPal

It is challenging to be entrepreneurial in a large company—managerial instincts are typically to protect the core and continue what made the company successful in the first place. But the most successful companies are those that disrupt themselves before someone else does. That's not easy! I've had some great opportunities to innovate in large media companies—like Nickelodeon, Dow Jones, and now at BBC Studios, where we have recently launched a new streaming service called BritBox—and I have learned a few salient things in the process.

First, a culture of innovation starts at the top. The CEOs of truly innovative companies are not afraid of taking risks. Some believe that if you're not failing at things, then you're not trying hard enough. They also hire diverse management teams—people who are different from them. When the CEO of Dow Jones hired me, he took a risk—I had a background that was markedly different from those of others on his senior team. But he wanted the company to change and grow, and knew he needed different skills to do that. I tell my team, "If we're finishing each other's sentences, then we will fail." **Conformity may feel comfortable, but different voices challenging the norm help creativity and lateral thinking come into the mix.**

Perhaps most importantly, a strong customer focus is key to successful innovation and growth. Knowing your customer may sound easy, but it is not. Customer insight is not just about an occasional survey or focus group. When I was at Nickelodeon, we conducted close to two hundred focus groups every year. We wanted to understand kids in all dimensions; not just what kinds of shows they liked, but how they felt about school, their friends, their parents, and life in general. That helped us to create shows and characters that kids could really relate to as well as a channel that made them feel like it was all about them. We then grew the Nickelodeon brand and business into other areas—like toys, apparel, live shows, and theme park attractions—leveraging our deep understanding of what kids liked and what they liked to do. While not every company can do two hundred focus groups every year, successful innovative companies have ways of developing a deep understanding of who their customers are and how to super-serve them in their business.

I have found some common characteristics among really innovative executives—they are curious, they are resilient, and they take on challenges that can feel risky or difficult. My best example of all three comes again from Nickelodeon, where I led a cross-functional "skunkworks" team of people who developed the initial business plan for the channel Noggin. We spent the better part of a year fleshing out the various dimensions of the channel, the brand, and the business, all while juggling our day jobs! Noggin successfully launched a couple of years later. That experience allowed me to demonstrate my leadership skills and helped me to develop skills in important new areas. Soon after, I was promoted from a strategy position into running a business.

For me, taking risks and embracing challenges have helped to grow the businesses I've worked on and my career as well, each step of the way.

4 COLLABORATE TO FIND YOUR SIDE HUSTLES

You have the same number of hours in the day as Beyoncé."

Whether you love or hate this quote, there is some truth to it. We all get 1,440 minutes a day, and while eight to ten of those hours may be dedicated to your job, you also have another fourteen hours that are all your own. Hours where you can be pursuing opportunities that are related to your dream job, expanding your network, and strengthening your resume and skill sets apart from what you do during business hours. Whether you call it your "after-hours" or your "side hustle," it is during those hours that are "yours" that you can take on roles that can become accelerators, and collaborate with people who could enable you to get to where you want to go much, much faster.

I know you may feel tired at the thought of devoting your "free time" to more "work." But the work that I have done in my side hustles was not only the most exciting, but the most energizing as well. It was these different roles outside my corporate job that led me to be one of *Forbes* magazine's "30 Under 30," unintentionally leading to the creation of Mogul. Because I took on multiple side hustles during my years at Yale, Credit Suisse, HBS, and CBS, I had established a deep portfolio of work and friendships, as well as opportunities that begot more opportunities.

On the path to achieve success and impact, you have to ask yourself:

What am I going to do for my side hustles? They can truly be your ultimate accelerator.

REACH OUT TO YOUR ROLE MODELS

The starting point for finding work to do in your after-hours is to think about people you know—people who are doing what you want to be doing, or working in the industry you aspire to join. Then reach out to see if there is a way for you to get involved in what they are doing. **You aren't looking for a job. You will most likely not get paid. You aren't looking for advice. You aren't looking to take something from them. Instead, you are investigating ways that you can continue learning outside regular business hours by helping *them*.**

And thanks to the power of the Internet, you don't have to live in a major metropolitan area to reach out to your role models. I didn't always live in New York either. Remember that I went to high school in Plano, Texas? My first real side hustle, at that time, was as the fan club manager for Kari Kimmel, a songwriter whose songs have been featured in hundreds of films and television shows, such as *The Office* and *Keeping Up with the Kardashians*. Even though she was based in Los Angeles and we had never met, I reached out to her over email to express my great interest in her work and ask whether there was anything I could do to support her. She said yes, without needing much more convincing; I could help manage her web presence and fan mail. Done. And with that, I had a mentor and friend.

Obviously, the ideal way to reach out to any potential mentor is using warm connections—when you have someone in common who can facilitate an introduction. But sometimes you don't have a warm connection. That's when you have to do a cold email. There's no way around it. But always remember that you have something of value to offer them. You are willing to help, with anything, for free. Stay focused on how you could help them (and not the other way around). **Let a spirit of generosity exude through your writing and you will receive a response more often than you expect.**

The Art of the Cold Email

Think of fifty different people in the industry that you want to work in who might have a side project that you could support in some way. Track down their emails by connecting with them through Mogul or LinkedIn, and then reach out. Here is a general script/guideline to follow.

1. Refer to their current role and genuinely express your interest in what they are doing or any recent successes.

2. Share how you'd love to hear about their latest initiatives and a bit about your own background that might provide a fruitful collaboration. Again, stay focused on the value you can bring to them.

3. Ask to host them for a fifteen-minute tea at a location and time convenient for them. Make it clear you are not going to monopolize their time. Suggest two dates and a window of hours on each date to help narrow down potential meeting times and give them something specific to respond to.

4. Thank them, sign off, and then, below your signature, include a short paragraph describing your background in more detail. This way, it won't crowd the body of the email.

This approach is still effective for me to this day and is one that I've passed down to many mentees and team members. My colleagues and I nearly always get a yes. That said, if we don't hear back, we don't get discouraged either. Everyone is busy, and if at first you don't succeed, wait one to two weeks and email them again. Resilience and tenacity always win. And stay focused on creating a feeling of wanting to give, wanting to support, and wanting to collaborate.

If you reach out to fifty people, maybe ten people will reply to you, two people will agree to tea, and one person will agree to collaborate. But that one person can change your life.

Here is an example of such an email.

Dear X,

It is a pleasure to meet you over email. I've heard wonderful things about your company and how it has been [something that shows you have been following them and are familiar with their accomplishments and work].

I've greatly admired your work in this area and hoped to further connect in person. I am the founder and CEO of Mogul, which collaborates with Fortune 1000 companies to create global impact on women worldwide [substantiate yourself with credibility]. I'd love to meet in person to hear more about your latest initiatives, and discuss ways in which we might be able to collaborate.

It would be an honor to host you for tea. Would you be available on Monday, November 1, between 10:00 a.m. and 12:00 p.m., or Wednesday, November 3, between 2:00 p.m. and 4:00 p.m.?

If neither of those times would work well for you, please feel free to let me know dates and times that would be more convenient.

Thank you and warmest regards,
Tiffany

When I was at Yale, one of my closest friends was a girl named Lizzi. She was two years behind me, but once I graduated, we stayed in touch and are still as close as ever today. While I was at Credit Suisse, creating financial models during the day, I visualized making further inroads into the media industry at night. Lizzi and I would frequently chat about life and family, including her father, who worked at *Saturday Night Live* and to whom she offered to introduce me when I was ready. But I was too shy to take her up on it. At last, though, I worked up the courage to ask if it would be all right. I messaged Lizzi, feeling a bit awkward, as I had never asked for an introduction from anyone before. I knew I had to do it, though. I asked her if she happened to know if her father or anyone else in the media industry might need some help? With anything? Ever the caring friend, Lizzi excitedly sprang into action and put me in contact with both her father, Rob, and her cousin Steven, who also worked in the industry.

I soon reached out to Rob, telling him about my background and my ultimate goals. I mentioned being the fan club manager for Kari, years prior. I said I was available to take on any kind of role, to help in any way he might need. He responded in short order, saying he was developing an off-off-Broadway musical called *Volleygirls*, and sent me the script for feedback.

I was so excited. Here was a real luminary in the industry, and he had just sent me a script! That evening, as soon as I got home from work, I curled up on my bed with a cup of tea, read through the entire script twice, and sent back detailed edits.

A few days later, I received another email from Rob. He was impressed with my initiative. Not only had I sent feedback so quickly, but I had really thought through my comments (in fact, I probably gave him way more edits than he was expecting). He ended the note by inviting me to a rehearsal for a read-through of the script.

I soon showed up at their family apartment, where he and his wife, Carol, warmly invited me in; he introduced himself and some of his collaborators who filled the room, including the producer of the show, Monica Raymund, a Juilliard graduate who went on to star on the NBC TV show *Chicago Fire*. After the rehearsal, Rob asked whether I might want to be the check-in girl once they started previewing the show in a theater. "Of course," I said, "I'm happy to do anything to help! Give me anything at all. I would love to do it!" I didn't know exactly what a "check-in girl" did, but I knew I would be more than happy to discover what the job entailed, and do it to the best of my ability.

A few weeks later, there I was, checking people in at *Volleygirls*. Now, while check-in girl might not sound like an important job, it was the coolest role to me because it gave me the chance to meet different producers, financiers, and potential cast and crew members who attended each performance. These were the people who could create enough momentum to actually bring the show to a bigger stage full-time. It was important that Rob knew each and every person who attended and had a way to follow up to see if they wanted to be involved. So during each performance, I sat there with my laptop and highly organized Excel spreadsheets, and not only took people's names but made sure I had their contact information as well as other useful background information, from extensive research I would do. This would allow Rob to be able to reach out afterward to gauge their level of support and interest. Rob would be able to leverage the right resources only if he knew exactly who came to the show and what they were bringing to the table.

After that first show, when I sent Rob my spreadsheets, he was thoroughly impressed. He'd never had someone take it to that level before.

He invited me back. And after a couple of weeks, Rob asked if I would want to be general manager of the show. Of course I said yes. I was twenty-two, working full-time at Credit Suisse during the day. And now I would have this incredible opportunity at night.

When you build trust and become someone's go-to person for any job, big or small, you can accelerate your path to the job you truly want.

Rob was and continues to be a wonderful mentor for me. Monica, too; she became the first member of our Mogul Think Tank. Collaborating with them opened countless doors. But I never went up to them and asked them to mentor me. And while I believe that having someone to model and learn from is key, I don't think a mentor should necessarily be someone who guides you along and provides advice to you. Ideally, I think a mentor should be someone with whom you collaborate, so that along the way, you learn from him or her and hopefully vice versa. When you approach a relationship with a potential mentor with the attitude of *What can I do for them?* instead of *What can they do for me?* you'll find that many more doors will open for you.

Determining What Value to Bring

When I was looking for side projects to develop my more creative skill set, including writing, I would Google "contributor positions in New York." It was in this way that I discovered that top-tier magazines were often looking for contributors to their publication online. I realized that writing articles for them would not only hone my writing skills, but also allow me to offer something of value to the people I was trying to build relationships with at the time. I would reach out, and offer to profile them online, providing exposure for them and their company, and giving me a chance to meet them one-on-one. I would then follow up after the article would run, and in part due to the goodwill that had been built between us, soon a friendship and collaborative relationship would emerge.

Your value could be something small, but important, like being a skilled calligrapher and offering to address invitations. Your value could be a love for Excel spreadsheets, and you could offer to reorganize their databases. Your skill set could be web design, and you could offer to work on their website or create ads for them.

But sometimes, just a willingness to step into any role is what is most needed. Offer your help broadly and see what they come back with.

DISCOVER THROUGH DOING

Around the same time that I became the general manager of *Volleygirls*, I connected with Lizzi's cousin Steven, an entertainment lawyer who had worked with countless stars like Lady Gaga and Britney Spears. By this time, Rob was singing my praises and knew that I would be just as indispensable to Steven as I was for him. Upon meeting, Steven was ready to give me something to do because both Lizzi and Rob had vouched for me prior. One introduction is great, but two is even better.

Steven was writing articles about the disruption of music

distribution, due to the emergence of streaming services like Napster. So he asked me to take a pass at editing his first drafts. I was happy to do anything and of course accepted. When Steven sent me the first article, I edited it thoroughly. He liked what I'd done and sent another one. Whenever he would send me an article, he would ask whether I could get it back to him in a week. But I often sent him the piece within twenty-four hours. Steven loved my initiative and drive, and began to involve me in more and more of what he was working on.

Not all of the work that Steven gave me was 100 percent relevant to what I wanted to do in the future. But I had the opportunity to learn, and that was what mattered. It allowed me to discover my strengths and passions through doing various tasks. You can't know if you truly love something unless you try it. Again, it is key in these relationships to be indispensable and willing to do any kind of task, big or small.

If your day job isn't your passion, use those extra hours to discover what it is you truly love to do.

And who knows what the next task they give you might entail? Because of Steven's track record as a thought leader in entertainment, others were always bringing him new opportunities to be involved in, whether it was a business venture, a film, or a new artist they were trying to launch. Steven started to invite me to attend these meetings and would ask me my thoughts afterward. In many ways, I was a sounding board for him. Someone he trusted to think about things in a logical way. But for me, every meeting was an opening to countless new doors. When he invited me into these high-level meetings, he allowed me to see how he weighed different options. When he invited me to meet various people in the media industry, at startups, and in entertainment, it was unprecedented access. It was invaluable.

And while it felt to me like he was doing this huge thing, I was also helping him. Leaders in any industry often have side projects that they barely have time for, and if you can become their go-to person to support them in these endeavors (for free), you learn a ton and continue to get more opportunities to serve, support, and learn.

One of my favorite things about Mogul is that we are working to break down the barriers to these kinds of collaborations. Mogul allows millions of women across the world unprecedented access to thousands of celebrities, CEOs, Olympic athletes, and other luminaries, such as Katie Couric, mayor of Paris Anne Hidalgo, Nina García, Kelly Osbourne, Margaret Cho, and Chelsea Clinton. Through our #AskAMogul series or daily interactions on our platform, women worldwide can ask any question about the life and career of their role models and vice versa. Mogul was created because I wanted everyone to have access to the kinds of relationships that can truly change your life.

CREATE THE OPPORTUNITY YOURSELF

Another way to find projects for your after-hours is to make sure that you are staying engaged in the industry you want to work in. Attend events, dinners, and conferences where you might have a chance to connect with people who could offer you rewarding opportunities to step in and help. When I was working at HBO between my years at Harvard Business School, one of the other MBA interns, Krystal, was working on the marketing side, and we would get together and share knowledge and laughs. One day, Krystal invited me to a film premiere that she was going to that night. The film, *Girlfriend*, had been directed by a college friend, and she looked forward to catching up now that they were both in the same industry. I agreed to attend as her "wing-woman."

I had never attended a film premiere before and was definitely out of my element at this very Hollywood after-party (despite it being in New York City) at Justin Timberlake's restaurant Southern Hospitality. There I was in a plain gray 1950s-style wool work dress while many of the other attendees were dressed to kill. I was surrounded by models, actors, and film executives, and let me tell you, I felt very out of place. There was a part of me that instantly wanted to leave. But I was deeply touched by the film. And I knew I needed to stay and speak with the film team, or I would regret it. It was the first North American feature film to cast a man with Down syndrome in the leading role. It was about this man's pursuit of a girl he loved, and it was just beautifully and wonderfully done. As I looked around, I recognized one of the producers, Jerad, standing at the bar alone.

I wanted to go up to him and tell him how much I enjoyed the film, as well as the Q&A he led after. Everyone likes to hear how his or her work impacted someone in a positive way, and this all had genuinely resonated with me. But I had to gather the courage to go up to him. This was a loud, high-energy party, and this was someone I didn't know. But Krystal and I had come to make friends, right? So why not seize this opportunity to do just that?

Nailing the Approach

Approaching new people is a skill that some people possess naturally, and other people have to hone. I'm someone who needed to hone this skill. For me, the biggest hurdle is often knowing what I am going to lead with. How am I going to get their attention? For this situation, it was pretty easy. I liked his film. Great. There's my first line. For other situations, the entry line may not be so apparent. You could try to find something to compliment: "I really like your bag!" Or make a comment about the setting you find yourself in: "This music is really loud, isn't it?" Then go ahead and introduce yourself. "Hi, I'm Tiffany Pham. I work at . . ." Now, some people don't really want to talk. At that point, you may get a turned back. That's fine. A little rejection will not ruin you. You can walk away knowing you tried. But sometimes it's good to have a second line as well, already prepared. "You work at [company name], don't you? I really love your app. I use it all the time to get food delivered to my office."

And thus a conversation is started.

Trust me, sometimes just knowing what exactly you are going to say is enough to get you over that hurdle of approaching someone. You are prepared. You are taking a chance. If they ignore you or don't really respond to your introduction, you can't take it personally.

As soon as I walked up, introduced myself, and told him how much I enjoyed his film, Jerad immediately and candidly shared the struggles they were having. The film, after premiering at the Toronto International Film Festival, had been bought by a distributor that had since folded. And because they legally held the rights to distribute the film, no other distributor could take it on; it had taken the producers of the film over a year to acquire back the rights for distribution. Despite being a groundbreaking film and having won numerous awards, this film had unfortunately had a stroke of bad luck. No one was going to be able to see it.

I couldn't imagine how disheartening it would be to have your project be well received by your peers, but then be essentially caught up in a legal no-man's-land. I wanted to help.

"I'm currently at HBO in distribution. Maybe there's something I can do? Or at least I could offer to show the film to my classmates at Harvard Business School in the fall? I'd love to do anything I can to help," I told him.

He looked at me in surprise. "That would be great, thank you!" And then he handed me his card.

I'm sure he never expected to hear from me again. But the next day I sent him an email with three specific ways I could be of service. They weren't big ways, but I wanted to follow up and make good on my promise to help. He responded shortly thereafter, saying, "Let's set up a call." And before I knew it, we were on the phone, and he said, "How would you like to help us with the actual distribution of the film?"

My heart was beating so fast, and in my head I was screaming, *Yes! I'd love to!* But on the phone I was cool as a cucumber. "Sure, no problem."

When I hung up the phone I ran over to Krystal's desk and said: "Krystal, how do you distribute a film?"

"I don't know," she answered honestly.

"I don't know either, but I'm going to have to learn!" And I told her about the conversation I'd just had.

There we sat in the cubicles of HBO, Googling: "How do you distribute a major feature film?" And despite the fact that Google often has an answer for everything, it wasn't that helpful with this.

I knew in that moment that I could fail. I didn't know how to do the job I'd just offered to do! But I thought of my father and his insistence that there is no failure as long as you are failing forward. True failure is not doing, not trying. **True failure is turning away from opportunity because you don't want to face your fear.** I thought of how much fear must have coursed through my parents' hearts as they picked up their lives to move to France. And then how much more fear faced them as they uprooted their three children and moved to Texas. But those steps were so important to their growth. Facing those fears led to a world of new opportunities. And here I was, in the middle of getting a degree from Harvard Business School, with the opportunity of a lifetime.

So yes, I was afraid. But I wasn't going to let that stop me.

Not knowing what else to do, I decided I would just call different theater chains across the United States and ask what it would take for them to show this film in their theaters. It would be time-consuming, I would probably get a lot of "nos," but it couldn't hurt to ask.

The first chain explained how things worked for them: "Oh, we'd do it for free, but with a cut of revenue." The next one said: "It costs [X amount], but you can take it out of the proceeds." The rest offered an entirely different setup.

I eventually determined which company had offered me the best deal and then went back to the others to see if they would agree to it.

And that is how I learned how to distribute a film. I didn't have a mentor. I didn't watch someone else do it. I said yes to the opportunity even though I had no idea what I was doing. But I trusted that I had the ability to learn.

Women notoriously don't apply for jobs until they meet 100 percent of the qualifications, while men are known to apply for jobs even if they are only 60 percent qualified. What if our hesitation, our unwillingness to risk failing, is one more thing that prevents us from moving up the corporate ladder? Here's my question: How can you learn unless you jump right in?

Always trust that you have the ability to learn.

When I called Jerad to tell him that I had different theater chains interested in showing the film, he couldn't believe it. He was so thankful and couldn't wait to share the news with his team. He assumed I made it happen because I had all this experience, when really, it just took a bit of gumption and the willingness to learn.

I eventually repeated this process, picking up the phone and pitching the film to major distributors who would be able to distribute the film beyond theaters, across all electronic platforms as well as international territories. Within a week, I was able to sell the film to a top-tier distributor. Again, to the team's disbelief. They had been told by Hollywood veterans that it couldn't be done; the film, the veterans had said, had been on the market for much too long due to the yearlong legal snafu.

My naïveté, my sincere lack of awareness of how the system actually operated, had worked in our favor. To quote the equally sincere Elle Woods, when she was asked in *Legally Blonde* how she got into Harvard, "What? Like it's hard?"

I subsequently helped with efforts on marketing, and the film ended up receiving a Gotham Independent Film Award, one of the biggest awards you can receive as an independent film. And in the fall, I brought the film to HBS for a special screening and Q&A with the producers.

The morning after the HBS screening, Jerad let me know, as a thank-you for everything I had done for the film, they wanted to credit me as coproducer on it.

I was shocked. But of course I graciously accepted. Here I was, twenty-four years old, now a coproducer of an award-winning feature film.

It was a pinch-me moment. One that led to many more pinch-me moments, as Jerad and the rest of the team shared with their friends all that I had done for the film. Soon I was approached by other directors and producers, with contracts in hand. As I became involved with the film production process from end to end, I could now check off "Content" from the checklist.

Now, normally, if you want to become a producer on a film, what path do you assume you need to take? Start as a production assistant maybe? Then work your way up to production coordinator, line producer, and production manager, and then maybe, after five to ten years, you can be a producer? I may have jumped to the top just by being in the right place at the right time, but I also saw the biggest need and offered my help to meet that need, simultaneously learning something new.

The "I'll Do Anything" Attitude

Much like when I was determining what full-time jobs to take after college and business school, I always tried to stay focused on what skill sets I still needed to develop, in order to one day be ready for my ultimate dream job. If your day job is providing a great background in finance, then think about how to exercise your creative side in your after-hours. Or if your day job is super-creative, see if you can find opportunities to develop skills in business management or marketing. Going in with an attitude of "I'll do anything" can lead to that open door. That is even more important than the task you are given to do.

COLLABORATE AS FRIENDS, THEN PARTNERS

One thing that has always served me well is that when I attend industry events like that film premiere, I don't think of it as networking, but as an opportunity to build relationships and make friends. When I went up to Jerad, I sincerely just wanted to tell him about my appreciation for his film. I reached out on a personal level to connect, and once we started talking, his need arose, and I offered to see if there was anything I could do about it. Again, I wasn't looking for a rung up or a producing credit. I was just focused on the person in front of me and how I might be able to help with a problem he was facing.

This attitude shift can be powerful. Instead of looking to "network" with people who could connect you to your next job—a relationship that is by its definition transactional—I recommend focusing on building relationships with like-minded people who could become collaborators, partners, and friends. Collaborating to learn new skills leads to friendship, which in turn leads to lifetime partnerships.

I first met Kevin when I was in business school. Originally from Beijing, he was pursuing a PhD in physics at Harvard, but his passion was international film production and distribution. Because of this passion, he soon met me through the Entertainment & Media Club at HBS that I was president of my second year.

Kevin and I became fast friends. Like me, he was entrepreneurial in spirit, and varied in his interests (I mean, a PhD in physics, with plans to become an international film producer?). I had recently finished working on the distribution for *Girlfriend,* and we would daydream about the different ways we might collaborate together someday. Kevin's family was well connected with the Beijing government. He knew there was immense funding available in China for film projects, and I knew firsthand how many U.S. productions were desperate for funding; I had by then become close friends with many talented screenwriters and filmmakers here in the United States. We knew there had to be a way to connect these two groups who had so much to offer each other.

It wasn't until a few months into my time at CBS that Kevin and I formally finalized our partnership. Kevin had recently been in touch with the vice mayor of Beijing, who told him that Beijing's State-owned Cultural Assets Supervision and Administration Office, which was responsible for investing toward the capital of China's continued cultural innovation, was interested in pursuing a screenwriting competition. A high-profile initiative, the Beijing International Screenwriting Competition would invite screenwriters in the United States to submit their screenplays, centered on Beijing as a location. Finalists would be given all-expenses-paid trips to Beijing, and ultimately cash prizes would be awarded. Even for those screenwriters who didn't receive the Grand Prize, the exposure they would attain from being a finalist could lead to important relationships that could lead to film financing. The goal was to cultivate continued creative dialogue between China and the United States and bridge the cultural gap.

This was exactly the kind of collaboration that Kevin and I had envisioned working on, and with the Beijing Municipal Government at the helm, I immediately agreed to be involved in cofounding the venture and serving as global head of marketing.

This was over a year after Kevin and I had first met. If I had approached my interaction with Kevin as a networking opportunity instead of as a true friendship and potential collaboration, I'm not sure that we would have stayed in touch over the time it took for the right opportunity to come our way. But because Kevin and I had become true friends, as valuable people in each other's lives, whether we worked together or not, we were still in touch when this opportunity arose and, as a result, he reached out to me.

Networking can be perceived as cold, transactional, and short-term. Collaboration is warm, focused on friendship and support, and can last for a lifetime.

This endeavor soon consumed most of my after-hours work. Kevin and I were on the phone every night, discussing the possible timelines for submissions, the guidelines we needed to establish, brainstorming who would be on the panel of judges, and what each step in the process might look like.

As global head of marketing, it was also my job to spread the word about this competition so as to get as many entries as possible from the highest-quality screenwriters. I managed a PR team to get the competition covered in *The New York Times*, *Variety*, *The Hollywood Reporter*, *Deadline*, and more—we got coverage in more than four hundred publications. I additionally collaborated with universities and film schools to spread the competition to students, as well as talent agencies to share with their clients.

In February 2013, the competition opened, and submissions

started streaming in. Kevin and I were thrilled with the response. We received approximately a thousand screenplays within days.

By the close of the competition, I had the honor of being one of the hosts for the awards ceremony at the Beverly Hilton, where the Golden Globes were typically held. Luminaries such as director James Cameron, Senator Elizabeth Warren, and former Governor Deval Patrick had supported the endeavor, writing us letters of praise and encouragement. We shared their remarks on how important this kind of intercultural exchange was for the artistic community.

As I stood on the stage, awarding each of the winners and their work, I watched the screenwriters' dreams come true. In that moment, I felt ready to be an entrepreneur. After all, Kevin and I had taken this simple idea, built the infrastructure to put it into motion, and made it a true success with global impact. Through this experience, in which I gained significant insight on branding and marketing, I began to believe more in myself: I could successfully launch and market a new venture.

If you are only willing to "work" during your office hours, you miss out on opportunities for so many fulfilling endeavors, and the ability to start having an impact, now.

Some of my best collaborators have been friends first, like Kevin, people whom I have met and connected with on a deep level. We are kindred spirits and are interested in the same kinds of endeavors. **Look for people who might come alongside you, become your partner, and allow you to accomplish more together than you ever could on your own.**

It is rare for me to work with someone just one time. I tend to work with the same people again and again. Those relationships beget more relationships that lead to more opportunities. Some of the people whom I invited to work on the Beijing International Screenwriting Competition ended up inviting me to work with them on various films. One was a powerful documentary called *Child 31*, focused on the important work being done by the nonprofit Mary's Meals. Based in Scotland, and founded by Magnus MacFarlane-Barrow, Mary's Meals was addressing two of the greatest needs in the world today: education and hunger. In poverty-ravaged countries in Africa, often the only place a child will receive a meal is at school. Mary's Meals commits to being that meal for children, not only so that they will fill their bellies and address this devastating health crisis (more than eighteen thousand children die per day due to hunger-related illness), but also so that children are encouraged to attend school, as a way to escape hunger. They serve more than one million meals every day.

Even though producing films was generally a "night-shift" job for me, doing so provided instrumental growth and learning, accelerating my ability to build my own company at the age of twenty-seven. Working on these films led me to receive invitations to join the boards and business committees of No Limits Media, the Provincetown Film Festival, and WNET New York Public Media, opportunities that led to even more collaborations and friendships.

This after-hours work also allowed me to feel like I was having a positive impact on the world, even when my day job wasn't necessarily as mission-focused as I was. My interest in production was never just about my love of films. (Though I do love films.) It was about the ability of the media to show us what is possible. All of the films that I worked on were not just artistic endeavors, but also highlighted different social issues that needed more global awareness. I realized that I had developed a pattern of working for a big institution during the day, establishing my reputation, and then doing all I could to give back at night.

Working on these films was a passion of mine, and something that gave me so much energy, even as I was working on them in my after-hours. Not only was I building skill sets and learning from influential collaborators, but I was doing work that truly filled my heart, and allowed me to know without a doubt that I was on the right path. That I would one day be able to combine the skills I was acquiring at CBS and the expertise I was developing on films, into one role.

As that day arrives for you, keep looking for opportunities to pour yourself into work that you care about and can learn from.

HOW TO GET IT DONE

So let's get down to the nitty-gritty. How do you find the time to do all of this while you have a full-time job?

I won't lie to you: It takes a lot of discipline.

If you have a job that truly sucks you dry, leaving you no juice for after-hours, maybe it is time to consider a career change. Because for me, even when I was doing exciting work during the day, I still had hours in the evening where I could be productive. I would be at CBS from 9:00 a.m. to 6:30 p.m., have dinner or attend an event after work, and then get home around 9:00 p.m., ready and eager to start my second shift. I would power up my computer, and stay focused between 9:00 p.m. and 3:00 a.m., when I would work on these projects that I deeply, truly loved. Without each one of these projects, Mogul would never have become what it is today.

I know that my former schedule won't work for everyone: going to bed around two or three in the morning, and then sleeping until six or seven, and getting to the CBS offices around nine. Yes, that meant I usually only got about four to five hours of sleep per night. That isn't sustainable for everyone. But if you are someone with a lot of energy, and a love of learning, you may embrace having a lot going on. It is good for your soul. It counteracts the tendency we sometimes have to waste our precious time. It means that you consciously choose not to spend your evenings binge-watching television shows, nor spend endless hours on social media. You will stay obviously connected to what is going on in the world and in your networks every day, but won't allow it to consume hours that you know could be productive.

Every night, after work, I review my list of projects currently under way. For each project, I think about the one thing that could most move that project forward at that moment. If each night I could accomplish that one thing, I knew each project would move forward. It's important to have the long-term goal, but not get overwhelmed by all the steps to get there. Stay focused on small goals and steps, ensuring that you are always moving things forward. Because these projects are just as much for relationship-building as they are for building skill sets, remember to take on just enough to be a superstar in each role, without letting your responsibilities overflow. Your reliability is key to establishing a bond with the others involved in the project, as well as strengthening your knowledge base concurrently.

The truth is, the work that you do after-hours is the stuff that makes you reenergized, not depleted. I can't tell you how many times I couldn't wait to leave class or leave the office and head home to do work that was even further firing me up at the time. Trust me, Yale was a great place to learn about economics and international relations. Harvard Business School was a great place to learn about general management. And my job at CBS was a great opportunity to learn about growing a business.

But those were never the only places I was learning. I underwent so much growth during my after-hours.

Once you hit the spot where you are finally working in the job of your dreams, your after-hours can be less focused on side hustles. Or if you aim to be an entrepreneur, you'll want to pour everything into your company if you've finally launched it. You'll take on less because you have narrowed down what you really want to accomplish and the skill sets that are necessary to build. But for those years when you are still trying to discover what you are meant to be doing with your life, or when you know what you want to do but still feel so far from accomplishing your goal, that's when these side projects are essential. They will help you reach your goal so much faster. You can save your sleeping for then.

#YouAreAMogul

Take advantage of your after-hours if you are still dreaming about your ideal job. Those hours are waiting for you to fill them with interesting connections, learning experiences, and opportunities that will open doors. Don't be afraid to teach yourself the skills you need to succeed. And recognize that relationships with people whom you respect, and who come to respect you, are the key to rewarding work and opportunities for advancement.

COURTESY OF TINA CHARLES

#IAmAMogul

By Tina Charles, two-time Olympic gold medalist, WNBA New York Liberty player, and founder of Hopey's Heart Foundation

As a professional athlete, I was always driven to achieve more and to not let my sport define me. I sought to do this by serving others in and out of my sport. Even though I've accomplished more than I could have ever dreamed in my career, it has never been the only passion of my life. Success, in my opinion, is the ability to impact someone else's life. Playing in the WNBA has its rewards; most important to me is the platform given to me and my peers to raise awareness on issues important to us.

Plus, my mother always told me: "You have a voice. Make sure you use it." I use my voice on the court, with my teammates. And I use it off the court to spread awareness about causes that truly matter. But it wasn't until April 2013 when I really crystallized what my cause would be.

My aunt, Maureen "Hopey" Vaz, was incredibly special to me throughout my life. She died in March 2013 of multiple organ failure. Hopey was known for having a very giving heart and, when her own heart failed, it was a tragic loss to our family and an eye-opener for me. Prior to her passing away, I read an article on a high school basketball player, Wes Leonard. Wes died of sudden cardiac arrest (SCA), when the heart suddenly stops. Having an automated external defibrillator (AED) on-site would have saved Wes's life. After being moved by the sad and sudden loss of Wes Leonard and my aunt's untimely death, I refocused my efforts to help reduce the chances of student athletes falling victim to sudden cardiac arrest. Mirroring my aunt Maureen's giving heart, the Hopey's Heart Foundation was founded in April 2013.

The Hopey's Heart Foundation was founded to prevent sudden cardiac arrest from claiming the lives of promising student athletes like Wes Leonard. The foundation offers grants to nonprofit organizations to purchase life-saving AED equipment.

Sudden cardiac arrest claims over 380,000 of hospital cardiac arrest episodes annually in the United States. The survival rate after an SCA decreases by 7 to 10 percent every minute without the use of an AED. But if the victim has the combination of an AED and CPR, there is a 75 percent increase in surviving an SCA.

Since starting in April 2013, to date, Hopey's Heart Foundation has placed more than three hundred of these devices throughout the world. I have personally donated my entire WNBA salary to Hopey's Heart Foundation, in order to keep communities' hearts safe.

And just this year, we saved our first life!

Mr. Dan Carlson, the head of landscaping at the Marbridge Foundation in Austin, Texas, a residential care facility for adults with intellectual disabilities, collapsed outside the gym on their 240-acre campus. Coworkers rushed to his aid, began to perform CPR, and called 9-1-1. They were instructed by emergency responders to use an AED, and one was available inside the gym thanks to the donation made in 2014 from Hopey's Heart Foundation.

Carlson was revived, survived the scare, and made a full recovery. I recently got to meet him. He expressed his gratitude and shared the fact that he is expecting to meet his first grandchild this year. It was an experience unlike any other. I've had a lot of highs in my life, winning championships and Olympic gold medals. But I've never had a moment like that.

It was amazing to see the impact that you can have if you just see a need and are willing to act. I give glory to God for putting it in my heart to start Hopey's Heart Foundation.

Whatever is in your heart, just do it. Just have the willingness to take that step. All I did was make a choice to do what I could about a problem that seemed avoidable.

And someone is alive today because of that choice.

It is not easy to balance my full-time career with the foundation and its growth. We are today seeking funding and finally looking to hire staff full-time. But at the end of every busy day, when I pack up to travel to one more place to raise awareness, I always know why I am doing this.

And it makes all the work worth it.

5 BECOME A MOGUL FROM YOUR BEDROOM

All those after-hours emails and late nights, and the times you put yourself out there, all those lessons learned, all those rungs up the ladder, they don't mean anything if you don't take the plunge when the time is right. You can keep doing your side hustles your whole life if you let them always take the back burner. At some point, you are going to be faced with a choice: Can I commit to making these side hustles, these things that I am deeply passionate about, my full-time job? Am I ready to realize that I have learned enough, interned enough, shadowed enough, and now it is time to step into the arena?

We are all faced with these moments.

And trust me, there are times when it isn't the right moment to jump ship, when you aren't truly ready, and it is best to wait. But sometimes those are just excuses. There are times when the invitation is there, and we can't seem to muster the trust in ourselves that we can do it. That we are ready.

It happened for me when I was twenty-seven years old. I had moved from my Sixty-Ninth Street one-bedroom apartment into a two-bedroom apartment with my younger brother, David, at Sixty-Seventh and Broadway, near the iconic Apple store. David was a tech prodigy, certified in multiple computer programming languages even as a child, a serial entrepreneur with several books under his belt. I greatly respected his philosophical insights coupled with his tactical wisdom from within the startup world. Beyond his intelligence, I also very much admired his exceptional calmness and generosity. We had always been each other's constant source of support, and hoped to spend more time together as siblings before both of us inevitably settled down with families one day.

Every night, I would look out onto the view from my balcony, where I would see the word "Empire" shining bright red from the Empire Hotel sign nearby. Though I didn't realize it at the time, that sign would become a nightly inspiration for me.

It was in that bedroom that the very thing I had been working toward since age fourteen was finally born.

It didn't happen overnight. In so many ways, all the little decisions that I had made up to this point led me to that moment. I began to feel that seed, that had been planted all those years ago, starting to take root.

I could have ignored the stirrings deep within. I could have kept busy with my day job. I could have come up with a million reasons why I was not the one to create the company I had envisioned.

But because I dared to dream, dared to believe that I was capable, I decided to teach myself how to code and build it myself.

I became a mogul right there from my bedroom.

ACCEPT THE INVITATION

Throughout the previous year, while I had been working feverishly at CBS, I had been dedicating my nights to the Beijing International Screenwriting Competition. As the global head of marketing, I'd been executing on our strategies, coordinating with schools, collaborating with talent agencies, and speaking with the press *a lot*. In addition, I'd taken on two more film producing roles during this time, including *Hermit*, a film being directed by my close friend Susannah (the one who had stayed with me during our college trip to Myrtle Beach). She had evolved into an exceptional director and was yet another example of a friend with whom I collaborated repeatedly through the years.

As usual, I had taken on these various jobs not for what they were paying me (which was oftentimes nothing), but because I had the opportunity to learn so much from each different role I took on. I felt like each one was an opportunity to learn new skills, meet new collaborators, and accelerate my growth. Each role was a step in the next direction toward that day when I would finally launch my own company.

But I had no idea when that day would come.

And then one morning, in January 2014, I woke up later than usual. I leaned over to grab my phone, and put on my glasses. As the screen came into focus, I saw a text from a former colleague named Scott, who had since moved into venture capital.

"Congratulations Tiffany!"

My heart started racing. I had no idea what he was referencing, but for him to reach out completely out of the blue, it must be something important.

I sat up and clicked on my email. I had hundreds of new messages. One was from a former HBS classmate. I read her email: "Tiffany! So excited that you made this list!"

And there was a link.

I immediately clicked on it.

I was listed in *Forbes* magazine's "30 Under 30," alongside Pete Cashmore of Mashable, David Karp of Tumblr, and Tavi Gevinson of Rookie.

Could I really be on here? Sure enough, there I was. A photo that they had gotten from my Facebook profile, with a paragraph about my job at CBS, the Beijing International Screenwriting Competition, and my roles producing films. I had no idea I was being considered. As you can imagine, then, I was floored.

News spread like wildfire. It was a whirlwind of a day, with more texts, emails, and calls from friends and family, thrilled for me and excited to celebrate. But what I didn't expect was the outpouring of support I received from people I didn't know, people who were curious about how I had found these various opportunities. Some people were interested in my work at CBS; some wanted to know about how I broke into the film industry; even more wanted to hear about my work with Beijing.

The email onslaught didn't stop after that first day. It continued day after day. I would come home from a full day at CBS to an inbox that was teeming with emails from people I didn't know, many of them from young women around the world who had located my email address online. They wanted to know what articles I was reading, how I'd gotten the three different jobs featured in the *Forbes* article, what resources I was accessing for opportunities.

Some wrote long emails from Asia, detailing the struggles they were facing living in cultures that didn't necessarily support the advancement of women. I learned about the term "leftover women," referring to any woman who was unmarried after the age of twenty-five. Women from the Middle East opened up about what it felt like when marriage was offered as the only acceptable, appropriate path for them. They marveled at the fact that I could seemingly go after professional success, without feeling any sort of stigma for not yet being married.

One woman from abroad wrote that she continued to dream about living a different life because she was an ardent fan of *Gossip Girl* and she loved all the possibilities that girls in New York had personally and professionally. *Gossip Girl* was a hugely influential and entertaining show, of course. But the fact that it had enabled this woman to begin envisioning a new life for herself made me think again about how influential the media can be. And how much more of the world I wished I could show her.

I was also getting letters from across the United States. With the many hurdles women still face for equal pay, equal acknowledgment, and equal access, I was receiving notes from women, from Chicago to Dallas, who wished, too, to strive for significance and success on their own terms.

From the very first message I received, I vowed to answer each and every single one. I had always hoped to create a company to empower women. This was my small way of beginning to fulfill that mission, even if it was just from my bedroom in the middle of the night.

Soon I began to receive responses to my emails, young women telling me that my letter had changed their lives. They told me they had received that interview, that promotion, or discovered a new opportunity due to the encouragement and advice I had provided. Every single time I read these notes, I would get goose bumps. This was the power of the Internet, that I could connect with these women who lived across the globe from me, that I could provide vital feedback that wasn't available to them where they lived, and that their lives would be changed for the better. I couldn't get enough of it.

It was then that I began to wonder: What if there was a site where millions of us all could share our learning among each other? A place for real discussions, real advice? Not just the graduation speech version of how we got various jobs, for example, but what we'd learned in yesterday's meetings and after work tonight? How we had failed recently, but gotten back up with our family and friends' encouragement? Most important, wouldn't it be better if all these women who were emailing me could also talk to each other? So that they could connect and help each other along the way? What if instead of sharing all of this information one-on-one behind the scenes, there was a platform for all of us to exchange our various advice and insights and ideas, from the ground level? Where we could come and help each other become that much better and stronger, together? In this way, we could realize our dreams, both personal and professional. What would it look like to create a place where women and men of all backgrounds came together in order to support women, lift up, connect, and encourage?

What if we created an online community where everyone was—or could become—a mogul?

Listen to the Whispers

There are moments in each of our lives where we are presented with an invitation to pursue something big. We can listen to the seeds of inspiration or we can ignore them and stay where we are. I encourage you to learn to listen. Sometimes you don't know what to do with those whispers. And that's okay. Just allow yourself to dream. What would happen if you did something about them? Think about one step you could take to start working toward the realization of that dream. Could you take a class that might give you a skill set? Could you reach out to a role model, and see what doors that might open? Could you connect with a like-minded individual and share your dream, and see if, putting your heads together, you might come to a solution or a next step that you could take together?

Allowing yourself to dream means listening to those inner whispers of longing. And seeing where they want to take you.

JUST GET STARTED

"Nothing will work unless you do," Maya Angelou has said.

I felt like I knew that there was an opportunity brewing and, if I worked hard enough, I could create the exact platform I was envisioning. The only problem was that I didn't know how to build a platform. And I certainly didn't have the funds to hire a team of engineers.

But I'd never let not knowing how to do something stop me before.

Not knowing is really an invitation to grow, learn, and evolve. Are you going to stay where you are? Or are you going to stretch out of your comfort zone and teach yourself how to do the very thing you don't know how to do? The only way I became a film producer was by being willing to take on jobs I didn't know how to do and vowing to learn how to do them, whether by Googling or by asking questions of everyone around me who might possibly know the answer. I didn't know what I was doing. But that had never stopped me. It shouldn't stop you.

It doesn't matter how you start, where you start, or why you start. All that matters is that you start. When you dare to try something new, it can be the foot in the door that leads to everything you've ever wanted.

I had recently published a book with my father and brother called *From Business Strategy to Information Technology Roadmap: A Practical Guide for Executives and Board Members.* I'm a huge nerd, I know. What does that even mean?

The book was written to teach organizations how to build out their technology infrastructure in order to bolster their overall business strategy. Based on that, I thought to myself: *If I was teaching others how to build their technology, why couldn't I build out the technology for this idea I was thinking of? If I was willing to take the time to learn how to code, I could build this platform myself.*

But teaching yourself how to code isn't easy, especially if you're not a very technical person, which I most certainly wasn't. Again, David was the tech prodigy of the family. I could have asked him for his help on coding, and it would have taken him probably a few hours. Seriously. But I wanted to push myself to be the one to actually create this platform, knowing its nuances inside and out. Deep down, I felt like this was probably the next step for me. The moment that I had been preparing for all my life when I would finally be ready to create something on my own. I wanted to start every part myself, so that I would know the difficulties of each aspect, never taking for granted the challenges that my potential future teammates might face.

But David did kindly provide me guidance. He recommended referencing a PDF called "Ruby on Rails Tutorial" by Michael Hartl, a step-by-step guide for how to download the necessary software and then build a website, as well as Q&A forums like Stack Overflow that were priceless resources when you ran into complications or problems. So, every day, I would go to my day job, then in the evening, work on my side hustles. Then around 3:00 a.m., the phone calls and the emails would stop. I'd make myself a cup of tea, clear the kitchen table, and teach myself how to code Ruby on Rails.

It took me an entire month to get through the first chapter (which was about how to download and set up the right software and tools, like Sublime Text and GitHub).

I'm not going to lie; those initial first steps were painful. And they may be for you, too. Don't get discouraged. Once I got through the setup and made it to the second chapter, I started enjoying myself. It was during the second chapter, when I began coding the very first features for the site, that it all became fun.

Push yourself to begin. Step up to the moment. The hard part is often just beginning, no matter what you're trying to do.

And thank goodness it was so fun, because my schedule became insane at this time. From 9:30 a.m. to 7:00 p.m., I'd be working at CBS. Then I'd get home and start my second job: producing films. I'd work on that from 8:00 p.m. to 11:00 p.m. Around 11:00 p.m., I'd respond to the various emails of the day asking for advice, trying to get to "inbox zero." And then from 3:00 a.m. to 5:00 a.m., I'd be teaching myself how to code.

Finally, at 5:00 a.m., I would put my phone on sleep mode, turn out the lights, and sleep until 9:00 a.m. I'd get up, get ready within ten minutes, get to CBS by 9:30 a.m., and do it all over again.

This grueling schedule wasn't easy to keep up. Did I always have time to do my laundry? No. Did I always go to work wearing matching socks? No. Did I have a lot of good hair days during this period? No. But was it worth it? Absolutely.

Page by page, I built a very basic website, which was initially a simple grid of pictures. Despite its simplicity, it had all the functionalities that I thought could help women from around the world connect and share what was most important to them, their real lives, their real selves. I didn't want this to be a static blog with random advice from me. I wanted this to be a living, breathing community, 100 percent user-generated, in real time. I wanted the focus to be on the women themselves; thus I wanted users to be able to upload content, and up-vote or down-vote it, so that on a real-time basis, you could see what was trending among women's conversations all around the world. To be able to see right now, in this moment, what was at the top of women's minds.

Of course, I didn't have any users yet while I was creating the platform. But without me even having to ask, my wonderful mother and father were already at their keyboards, spending time on the site, providing feedback as test users. My sister, Kym, a creative genius and renowned travel photographer with a worldwide following across her social channels, provided me with the initial photos that I could use for the site's design.

From the very start, I knew what I wanted to call the platform. Back in business school, I had had a nickname. My friends would call me "the media mogul" around campus as a term of endearment, given all my work in the industry.

But as I Googled the term one day years later, I was astonished at how rarely the word "mogul" was used to describe females. There were just a few names that were linked with that word within the search results. Oprah was one. Yes, of course, no argument there. Beyoncé was another. And also Sheryl Sandberg, Melinda Gates, Marissa Mayer, and Sara Blakely, founder of Spanx.

The sparse list of women ended there. Men easily made up the top search results. Warren Buffett. Jeff Bezos. And so many more.

It was at that moment that I knew I had to call the platform Mogul. I wanted to change the connotation of that word. I wanted the word to be attributable to men and women both. **Women are moguls, too. We are risk-takers, dreamers, and doers. We can set a goal and accomplish it and then some. The world just hasn't been noticing.**

But, of course, the domain "Mogul.com" was already taken (probably by a man! Actually, I met him at a friend's dinner recently, and he's very nice). So I bought the domain www.onmogul.com. I envisioned that, one day, when people were talking about something they had read on the platform, and someone asked where they had read it, they would come to say, "On Mogul."

I knew I was getting closer to being ready to put this out into the world. I had first started receiving emails in January. It was now June. There were so many ideas I had for how the site could grow. But I knew that I had time to build that out. I didn't want to get stuck trying to perfect the platform. I'd seen many friends or colleagues with a brilliant idea who were too afraid to put something out there that wasn't perfect. And so time would pass as they pursued perfection, instead of recognizing that your prototype needs interaction with the world to perfect itself. I'm a strong believer that you need to put your idea out there as quickly as possible. Do as much as you can with your rapid prototype, but know that you will be able to iterate toward perfection as you go. What I think is much more important than a perfect prototype is a proof of concept. Make sure that your concept is strong, targeted, and specific, and that you have a way to prove its worth. That is 100 percent more important than a perfect prototype of a concept that is only 50 percent there.

Mogul was just a simple platform to start, a place for women to connect and share information. I knew, in my mind, there were so many ways that it could grow, with partnerships and additional resources outside the platform. But what mattered first was, would the women come to it? Would they connect, would they share, would they be encouraged? Had they been looking for something like Mogul all along? That was the concept that was important to convey. The rest could come with time.

My "launch" plan was simple: I planned to send an email to the thousands of women who had reached out to me since the *Forbes* list ran. I figured hopefully they would pass it along to their friends, start using it, and the platform would grow over time. I certainly had huge hopes for it becoming a true destination for women across the globe. But I thought it would take quite some time for it to grow. I had heard that another site called Upworthy had been run by a remote team for its first two or three years. As a result, I 100 percent assumed I'd be a one-woman Mogul team, working out of my bedroom for at least the next two years.

Finally, I felt like the platform was ready. It was about midnight on a warm summer night. I pulled out my personal computer and jumped right into work on Mogul, knowing that I wanted to send it out by the end of the night.

I carefully drafted an email to these women, sharing what I hoped this site could be. I included the link. I pressed send. And then I waited.

Finding the Confidence to Take a Leap

Ever since I was a young girl, I've had this inner voice that emerges whenever I feel afraid to take a chance. I say to myself: 1) What do you have to lose? If you succeed, it will be such an amazing opportunity! and 2) If you don't do this now, you'll regret it for the rest of your life. And I never want to regret anything.

So I've had the tendency to push myself to do something, even when I'm afraid. I think about the fact that if I am fearful, that's yet another reason to do it. I *should* do it *because* I'm afraid.

PROGRESS, NOT PERFECTION

In the middle of teaching myself how to code, while still ruminating on the ideas I had had since age fourteen, I decided to resign from CBS.

By this time, all of my other projects had come to a natural end. And though it may have been risky to let go of that steady salary, there was something about how passionately I felt about coding that made me 100 percent positive that this was the next step for me. I didn't want to only devote a few hours a night to it. I wanted to give it my all.

I had never resigned from anything before in my life, as most of my internships and jobs had had natural timelines. I had difficulty leaving anyone or anything, in general, because of my deep loyalty to those in my life.

But when would be the right time, if not now? There is never a "perfect" time to start living your dream, and for me, it was either now or never.

I wasn't married. I didn't have kids. I could live on dollar packs of ramen noodles if I needed to. So what did I have to lose?

My father had always taught me that "money was freedom." But he'd also always said that starting a business and taking your future into your own hands was a lot less risky than working for someone else and putting your future in their hands. Sometimes you had to trust that with all your passion, dedication, and hard work, the money would come. I knew that this was my chance to control my own fate and build financial independence through my own hard work, while hopefully creating a global impact, reaching women across the world.

So I resigned. I knew that I needed to rip off the Band-Aid. And luckily, my superiors were incredibly supportive of me. We made a sweet and memorable pact to reconnect in five years at the Modern restaurant inside the Museum of Modern Art, where we could talk about all that had transpired during our days at CBS and all that had happened since.

I launched Mogul thereafter. I crossed my fingers and hoped for the best.

Within three days of launch, I noticed something unusual within my charts of analytics. We had reached more than a hundred and fifty thousand people. Something viral was happening.

Within six days, we reached five hundred thousand people.

By the next week, we had reached nearly a million people, becoming one of the fastest-growing platforms for women.

I couldn't believe it. I scoured the site, and read about the women who had joined. There were already so many comments being posted, and I responded to each and every one. I wanted to know who these women were and why they had connected to something that had until recently existed solely in my head.

Here is what they shared:

I'm from Pakistan—here, a girl's life is all about marriage. But Mogul helps me out by proving to them that we are more than what they say. Now, I'm kind of a feminist, and I love, love, love this Mogul.

Kanza

My biggest dreams are female empowerment, especially coming from a culture in the Middle East where that falls by the wayside. It's a joy to be a part of such a hearty and established program.

Stephanie

Women are helping to change the world, but many still face challenges with self-esteem and confidence. Mogul allows everyone to help these women see their true inner beauty.

Candy

I would've fainted, but I was too excited to read what they were saying and dive into all that they themselves had begun to post.

Mogul wasn't going to have a soft launch after all.

I felt justified that I didn't wait until everything looked perfect before I sent Mogul out into the world. The design of Mogul was incredibly simple at the start. But I was proud of it. Its design didn't matter; its message did. And it was connecting with people from the very start. The users themselves were able to jump right in and start connecting, and we were able to perfect its design in time. It may have looked simple, but it was fueled by the power of women connecting with other women. And nothing is more powerful than that.

Melinda Gates recently tweeted: "Take it from Tiffany Pham. **If you want to build a perfect business, start with an imperfect idea.**" I'm so honored by those words. But it has been true for me, and I share this with you in the hopes it will be true for you. I was willing to put something out there that was still essentially being developed, and Mogul's interactions with its users and the world allowed it to evolve into the Mogul it is today.

Make Others Your Motivation

One thing that has always kept me motivated, even when I'm tired and overwhelmed, is thinking about the people my work will benefit. For example, Kym, David, and I made a childhood promise to each other to buy our parents a new home one day. We saw how much they had sacrificed for their children, and we always felt motivated to do this for them as our gift and thank-you for their unending love and sacrifices. I was always saving pennies and quarters because I wanted to honor what they had given me. That was more important than any trinket I might find at the toy store.

Mogul was the same way. I was so focused not necessarily on how I would build this company, but on how this platform might help these women who were already reaching out to me, that I worked through those late nights, inspired and energized. It didn't matter how tired I was; there was more to do for them, and I couldn't wait to get to it.

DARE TO DREAM

Those million people, women who had found Mogul and fallen in love with it so quickly, helped further confirm for me that building this company was my destined future. I jumped right in. From that first day, I was perched cross-legged on my bed, pillow over my lap, laptop on the pillow, in my pink pajamas, working harder than I had ever worked before. I barely left my room. Truly. I would frequently go for a run first thing in the morning, at 6:30 a.m., but that was pretty much the only time I left the apartment all day. I didn't watch TV. I hardly ate. I barely slept. All I could do was focus. But I so loved what I was doing, it didn't feel like work at all.

My parents had come up from Texas and stayed with my brother and me during those first few relentless months, to provide their endless support as I embarked on the journey ahead. When I would emerge from my room around 8:00 p.m., they would be lovingly waiting with warm bowls of Vietnamese phở. I would hardly have an appetite, but they would encourage me to eat and remind me that even moguls needed time to rest in order to think. After that, I would head back into my room and continue working until 5:00 a.m., when I would finally allow myself to sleep.

I hadn't saved up much of a nest egg. In fact, I started Mogul with just two hundred dollars in the Mogul bank account. But I'd done the math and I knew that based upon our reach, we could start making advertising revenue on the site right away. Can you guess who our very first client was? Soraya, from York Street Noodle House in New Haven. As you will recall, she had been my first advertiser at *The Yale Herald* and had grown into a loyal friend through the years. When I told her about Mogul and our mission, she believed in it immediately and bought our first marketing campaign, without question. The next five hundred dollars in the Mogul bank account came from her.

And that was the start. Mogul was now not only making money, but immediately profitable. Though with a one-person team, that wasn't hard to do!

Small Decisions Can Have a Big Impact

There were two decisions I made on this early iteration of Mogul that I believe helped us to grow. For one, I went to a website called AddThis.com and got embeddable widgets that encouraged sharing of content. So any time a user scrolled down on Mogul, there was an invitation to share what they had read on social media. I believe this led to its viral explosion. For every million visits, there would be 650,000 social shares on average.

I also talked about Mogul to anyone and everyone I would meet, never shying away from reiterating our mission and vision. I would share what it was I was working on next and would be surprised at how frequently this turned into an offer of help and support from the person I was with. They, too, were very passionate about this mission, and wanted me to meet their friend at X company, or their past manager who was now an investor.

Did I know the exact path that Mogul was going to take? Did I know that I'd actually be able to code something myself, that it would work, that people would respond to it?

Not at all. I had no idea where it was going to go. But I had a gut feeling that this was what I was supposed to be doing, that this was an opening into the rest of my life, that this would be an incredible journey worth taking—to learn, to build, and to put it out there.

Now, one more thing. I get asked all the time: Is coding essential for women to know? In response to this, I can only tell you how it worked for me. It wasn't too dissimilar from the experience Neo had in the Matrix. Once he could see all that code for what it was, he was never the same and his purpose in life was beautifully and elegantly clear. That's how I felt when I built Mogul.

Learning to code changed my life. If I hadn't learned how to code, I wouldn't have understood our product nearly as well. I wouldn't have had such an intimate knowledge of our users and what they loved. In those early days, I was so deep into the machinations of the site that I was making tiny adjustments all throughout the day. Knowing how to code myself allowed me to respond to user feedback in real time. It allowed me to evolve the platform in essential ways every single day. That close-up view of what users responded to helped me to quickly refine over time toward what Mogul has become.

And it came to mean a lot to our users that I'd initially built Mogul myself. For them to know truly that they could do the same. That life was in their control. Opportunity was theirs for the taking.

You just have to be willing to step on board, and get ready for the ride of your life.

#YouAreAMogul

You can wait for someone else to solve that problem. Or you can look at your own very capable hands and realize that this is the moment that you've been waiting for. You are the one who can solve it. There will be sacrifices along the way. Sleep for sure. But there is nothing more satisfying than accomplishing something that once seemed daunting and impossible, entirely on your own.

#IAmAMogul

By Debbie Sterling, founder and CEO of GoldieBlox and *Time*'s "Person of the Moment"

As a girl obsessed with princesses growing up, it never even occurred to me that engineering was something I would enjoy. In fact, the first time I even thought about it was my senior year of high school, when my math teacher encouraged me to pursue it in college. Engineer? I pictured someone conducting a train.

But I gave it a try when I went to Stanford, and, four years later, I graduated with a degree in Mechanical Engineering/Product Design.

Unfortunately, I was one of the only women in my program.

I knew we needed to do something about this. And I decided I wanted to "disrupt the pink aisle" with a toy that would introduce girls to the joy of engineering at a young age. I created GoldieBlox.

I never set out to become a toy developer. **But sometimes you have to follow life's inspirations as they come, and explore their meaning.** This was a way in which I knew I could impact girls at a young age. Sure, I could be one of the few women in engineering jobs at a company. But who would really see me? I knew my impact could be greater if I started to show girls right from the beginning that they could build things themselves. To remind every girl she is more than just a princess.

In developing our character, Goldie, and her diverse group of friends, our goal was to create strong, female role models who have grit and are fueled by failure, yet still fun and relatable for girls and boys alike. The toy has now spawned books and a YouTube series. One of my favorite moments in our series is when Goldie takes apart an old car charger and uses its guts to build a DIY phone charger. As she pulls out the circuit board, she assures the viewers that these wires can seem intimidating at first, but they're actually super simple! That's the message I want to send through this show—let's not intimidate kids with engineering; let's empower them and encourage them to tinker, maybe mess up a few times, but ultimately use their creativity to become the makers and problem solvers of tomorrow.

It's okay to be a princess, but I want GoldieBlox to let every girl know she can build her castle, too.

6 ACCELERATE YOUR SUCCESS WITH THE RIGHT PARTNER

I left something out of that last chapter.

You know that empowering, exciting story about finally realizing my dreams and at last building a company that could help millions of women around the world?

Well, the week I launched Mogul was also the week that my boyfriend and I broke up. We'd been dating three years.

The highest of highs married with the lowest of lows.

The writing had been on the wall for a while, but I didn't want to see it. Of course, now I look back on it, and I'm thankful it happened. During a period where I had a lot going on, the biggest job of all was being his girlfriend, as he was upset that we did not live together at this time and wanted me at his apartment every day. When we broke up, I poured myself into Mogul and never looked back.

That said, I don't think you have to sacrifice love to have a career. I think that having a partner who can support you in your endeavors and vice versa can be the greatest gift. **The ideal is to have someone who is a partner in the truest sense, so that you are pushing each other forward, supporting each other's dreams and allowing each other to dream even bigger because you are by each other's side.**

DO NOT GET MARRIED UNLESS YOU FIND THIS

Who you choose to be your life partner is just as important as who you decide to have as your business partner—it can make or break your success. There have been studies from HBS about the disturbing disparity that arises between the success of HBS male graduates and the success of female graduates. Despite the fact that some people liked to blame this disparity on the fact that women chose to "opt out" for a few years when they had children, the studies were clear that it wasn't motherhood that prevented women from reaching their career goals. Many of them were still working full-time and always had. It was the lack of supportive husbands that led women to have less career success. Husbands still expected their career to come first and expected that any childcare or household issues were something their wife needed to handle, even if she had a high-powered career as well.

The headline in a recent *Harvard Business Review* article put it starkly: "If You Can't Find a Spouse Who Supports Your Career, Stay Single."

The choices that we make in our romantic lives are just as important to our eventual success as the choices we make in our careers.

I've certainly made some terrible choices along the way. The fact is, I didn't know what I needed until I had three relationships, one after the other. But as we've discussed, it's not really failure if you learned from the experience. This is especially true when it comes to relationships. I know that each relationship that I have had has taught me what I need, what is a deal-breaker, and what will ultimately serve me in the long run.

As you can tell by now, I don't worry easily. I typically have things under control. But the area of my life where I experience the most anxiety is my love life. Because it is the one area of my life that I cannot control.

One of the first viral posts I posted as a user myself on Mogul was called "DO NOT GET MARRIED Unless You Ask Your Partner These 15 Questions. Or Else You'll Wish You Had." Looking back, I didn't mean to sound so ominous. I suppose the breakup was still fresh on my mind. The post was about an article I'd read in *The New York Times* that really resonated with me on the heels of the breakup. It encouraged asking questions of each other like: What are your goals, and are you willing to adjust them for the relationship? What's your relationship with your family? And, why do you want to spend your life's journey with me? The post reached more than 11.5 million views. I wasn't alone in trying to navigate the rocky path of relationships and heartbreak.

That post was so powerful to the Mogul community because it reminded us to bring both our heads and our hearts into the equation. As women, we tend to lead with the heart, and sometimes the head gets left behind. I now strive to keep both involved, just like I do with any job I pursue, though I admittedly will always lead more with my heart. Does he light me up and fill me with passion? Great. But I also try to think about the practical side as well. Are we building each other up? Does it feel like we are truly partners? You will find yourself having stronger relationships when you bring your head into the equation as well. We must make smart decisions about who will be by our sides as we pursue our dreams.

Here's what I've learned in my "failed" relationships about what I, and perhaps you, need going forward.

SHARE ALL PARTS OF YOU

My first serious relationship took place shortly after college graduation. I met W at a Yale birthday party in New York City that he and his friends from Princeton had crashed. One of his friends liked my friend, and we were their wingman and wing-woman, respectively. While our friends didn't end up working out, we did, and we were together for many years. W was often likened to actor Robert Pattinson. Handsome, charming, athletic, and smart. He had been such a popular guy at Princeton that the shy girl inside me was stunned he could like me. But there was one major problem in our relationship. I was so concerned with always (*always*) being the perfect girlfriend to him that I wasn't actually being myself. I would *give, give, give*, and I didn't share how I was really feeling if I was ever upset or disappointed by something. We never fought, and that was something we were really proud of at the time. But now I see it was because we weren't telling each other what was truly going on. **Conflict is a crucial part of communication and connection. If you aren't openly addressing your conflicts, you aren't truly communicating and connecting.**

And that's the thing about trying to keep up with appearances and not being your authentic self: it can never last. When I moved to Boston for business school, we broke up, seemingly due to the long distance, but more likely due to a connection that was only skin-deep and could have been so much deeper. I never really knew what was going on with W, and I don't think he really knew what was going on with me. This became abundantly clear when we rekindled things about a year after having broken up. W had told me early on in our relationship that he had only cried once in his life, during the film *Ray* (strange, he knew). But he began to cry for the second time ever as he told me why he felt we had truly broken up a year before.

"Every time I saw you being successful, it ate away at me."

I looked at him in shock. I couldn't believe that my dear W could feel that way. As soon as he said those words, I knew. This could never last. I knew that the person whom I was meant to be with would never be undermined or hurt by me being who I am.

GROW IN THE SAME DIRECTION

Then came the relationship that I was in when I launched Mogul.

S, too, had gone to Princeton. S was charming, athletic, and smart, just like W. He was more introverted, but had a tight-knit group of friends from high school and Princeton, which coincidentally included W. Thus, when S and I started dating, it caused a rift in their friendship. In some ways, I think that S was overly invested in making the relationship work because of his competitive nature. In hindsight, he was likely more in love with the *idea* of me.

Within three weeks of dating, S told me that I had to be his girlfriend. Within two months of dating, S told me that he knew I was the one. He swept me off my feet initially, with these grand gestures. By our first anniversary, he had begun shopping for engagement rings at Tiffany's.

But soon he was forcefully pushing for us to move in together. I needed more time. I wanted to let the relationship continue to grow at its natural pace, in order to flourish. When I asked if we could possibly set a pace that was more in tune with both of us rather than this constantly accelerated pace, he seemed to understand, albeit with hints of bitterness and resentment. From that moment onward, things didn't seem quite the same.

We should have ended things right there. But we didn't. We dated for another two years.

It is hard when you are in a relationship, even a relationship that is not working, to figure out when to pull the plug. You get caught up in the comfort of having that person there, and the routines you've established. Plus, we *did* have fun. S and I would discover new parts of the city together: a speakeasy in the West Village that had no sign on the front door, or karaoke clubs in Koreatown with our friends at all hours of the night. I stayed focused on the occasional good things and tried to brush aside the increasingly bad.

Then, in 2014, S applied to business school. I offered to help him with his application—but he refused to let me. Instead, he made it a competition: "If you got into Harvard, I can get into Harvard. I'm going to get in on my own."

He had become dead set on matching or exceeding me in every way.

When he wasn't accepted, there was an immediate chill in our relationship.

Shortly thereafter, instead of being supportive of what I was doing, S would scoff at me. Friends would come by and be shocked to hear him mock me and taunt me for trying to teach myself how to code. He'd roll his eyes if others talked about my coding and mimiced me typing, hunched over a pretend keyboard.

I'm shocked looking back on it that we lasted after those demeaning gestures.

The night that Mogul went live, I went over to S's apartment. I was so invigorated with what I had just done, so excited that I had reached this new phase in my life and firmly convinced that this was everything that I had always dreamed of. Of course I wanted to share it with S.

Instead of being supportive, he was angry. Angry that I had quit a good job for what he considered a pipe dream, unlikely to succeed. It was devastating to be on this high, accomplishing this goal you'd always held for yourself, and the person you love and who you hoped would cheer you on can't even muster an ounce of happiness.

A few nights later, we finally broke it off for good. This is what he said to me as his parting words: "I don't think I can be with an R."

R was the CFO of a major investment bank, and her husband was the founding partner of a law firm. R had been a kind of second mother to S, and as a result, we got together with their family every month. They were a true power couple, with three sons, and they seemed to have it all, though, of course, I'm sure they had their occasional issues. Overall, they had a great family life, rewarding careers, the whole shebang. Through the years, we had often marveled at their kindness and generosity, with S contemplating that their family structure was what we should aim for. We would have our fulfilling careers, and together we would build a great family life while encouraging each other to achieve our dreams.

So when S said that to me with sadness in his eyes, I knew he had changed. He no longer wanted an R; he no longer wanted a true partner. Me.

So what went wrong? Since the moment he had met me, he knew I was someone who was kind and loving but also driven, with goals and dreams. How could he have changed his mind about wanting a woman who wanted a career?

I believe it's because he stopped going after what he really truly wanted.

S loved to write, and when we first started dating, he imagined being a comedy writer one day, or if not a writer, a teacher of some kind. Those were the kinds of jobs that truly made him feel alive, and I was hopeful he would pursue them. The problem? Those aren't super-lucrative fields, at least initially. So somewhere along the way, S convinced himself that finance would be the right path for him.

That was the fork in the road that meant the end of us. Because when S saw me going after my dreams, and having success, it reminded him of how much he was sacrificing in pursuit of money.

And so he stopped being supportive. He decided he wanted a more traditional partner, someone who would fit the mold within the new, more stoic life he had determined for himself. While I don't remember everything about the conversation that night, I do remember he kept talking about how he wanted someone to stay home, do the dishes, and walk the dog. And then, he essentially gave me an ultimatum: choose him or Mogul.

You all know which one I chose, brokenhearted. And it was the right choice.

If your partner can't get behind you having a career of your own, having goals you want to accomplish that are outside of being a support system, there is no need to waste any more time and energy in that relationship. If you follow your dreams, you will find someone to come alongside you who supports you along the way and vice versa. If your partner is not encouraging you in your endeavors, if your partner is not a cheerleader, sounding board, and confidant, find someone else. As Reese Witherspoon recently put it: "Run away from a man who can't handle your ambition. So many men think ambition is sexy!"

Those who express disdain for ambitious women are those who feel insecure. And nothing is less attractive than insecurity. If someone doesn't feel secure in his or her own identity and purpose in the world, he or she will see a woman with ambition and confidence as a threat. They may look to diminish you and your goals because they cannot stomach you achieving more success than them, even if you yourself care more for their love than this success.

So those signs of insecurity are huge red flags. Don't ignore them. Trust that this person isn't yet ready to be with you. That they need to feel confident in themselves and where they are going, otherwise they may only try to bring you down.

If you want your relationship to succeed, you have to be with a person who not only supports your passion but also, at the same time, is pursuing his or her own. This enables you to grow in the same direction, and then you can cheer each other on along the way. Otherwise, if you are headed in opposite directions, you'll always feel alone, isolated, and unable to reach them until it's too late. Work and relationships may seem like separate subjects, but they are greatly intertwined, especially for women. If your work is important to you, choosing a partner who supports your ambitions is absolutely crucial to fulfilling your dreams.

GET SOMEONE WHO GETS YOU

My last love, several years after S and I broke up and I launched Mogul, was primarily long-distance. T and I had been friends for years. And despite the fact that long-distance has its challenges, I learned to truly be myself and open up to someone in a way I never had before, perhaps because he already seemed to like me for me. I communicated with this man in a way I never had in my other two relationships, where I spent a lot of time with them and we did a lot of things together, but we didn't share a deep, passionate connection. Meanwhile, T and I, with our parallel backgrounds and interests, were able to come together in an intellectual and emotional way that I subsequently identified as being truly rewarding and nonnegotiable in all relationships going forward.

"Tiffany, when we are one-on-one," he once asked me, puzzled, "why don't you talk about yourself or your successes with Mogul more?" It was then that I knew this was the kind of man that was right for me. After years of being with others who discouraged and belittled me and around whom I would therefore downplay everything, this man encouraged me and was proud of me.

A successful, handsome businessman and entrepreneur himself, he was a dreamer, too, and absolutely pursuing his passions, and thus was not intimidated by me or competitive for my time. T taught me to really look for someone that I admire and respect, someone with whom I have a deep emotional connection, not just someone who is nice and easy to get along with.

Ultimately, we were on different life paths and separated by geographies, so next steps for us are unknown at least in the short term, but I will always be grateful that he showed me that it is possible to be with someone who totally gets you for you, who doesn't want you to change or dampen your passions, and who will support your dreams as they go after their own.

As you build your career, you are likely going to be searching for the right partner to come alongside you. But don't sacrifice your career, and what you truly want to accomplish in life, to accommodate someone you love. As Lady Gaga says: "Some women follow men, and some women follow their dreams. If you're wondering which way to go, remember that your career will never wake up and tell you that it doesn't love you anymore."

I couldn't say it any better.

#YouAreAMogul

Who you choose to be with is an important component to your career and life, and finding a partner with whom you can truly be yourself and who supports your dreams wholeheartedly, is essential to long-term success, of your career and relationship. Don't be afraid to be ambitious and hold firm for someone who loves that ambition as much as they love you.

#IAmAMogul

By Rebecca Minkoff, fashion designer and judge on _Project Runway: Fashion Startup_

I started my company when I was just twenty-one. I didn't know necessarily what I was doing, but I was driven and committed and willing to do what it takes. I didn't have much time for dating. When you start your own company, it seriously demands all of your time for a while. Until you build up a team to support you, you are the one doing every aspect of that company. So it meant that I didn't have a lot of opportunities for relationships.

Still, I so wanted to find someone to love. I knew I wanted a family, kids, the whole shebang, even though my company was truly my first baby. As a result, back then, I sometimes chose someone "being there" over someone _being right_. I had relationships that did not support me at all. Relationships that, looking back, I question _what on earth I was thinking!_

Then I met my husband, and it was like, _oh, this, this is what love is._ Everything I had been dabbling with in the past was a cheap imitation. Why did I waste so much time pining over that guy? This was the real thing. We dated long-distance the entire time, so that by the time we were actually married, it was so refreshing and invigorating to just get to be with him.

And he was totally supportive of my career. He knew that my company was incredibly important to me, that it was sometimes going to require all my time and energy, and that he would take the back burner. Not always, of course, but at times. He didn't feel threatened by that, and he always gave me the space to commit to my company.

Once we had children, we had to navigate entirely new terrain. We had to reorient our partnership and figure out how to navigate what our lives would look like now that we were parents.

I have the kind of career where twice a year, during Fashion Week, my family is just not going to see me. My husband is going to have to step up during that time. And he does, without complaint.

There are also times when I take the lead with parenting. We don't buy into the old-school thinking that Mom has dinner on the table and Dad works late. **The only way I can make my job work is to have an incredible partner,**

someone who is willing to value my career and my goals as equal to his own.

He makes it possible for me to have the very full life I do, filled with love, kids, and a kick-ass career. Don't ask me about work-life balance. I always say I'm not balanced, I'm juggling. But I'm so grateful I have the opportunity, and someone who forgives me and loves me anyway even when a ball inevitably crashes to the ground.

7 PITCH YOURSELF AND YOUR BIG DREAM

The weeks and months that came after the initial launch of Mogul were critical to making sure that Mogul thrived on a solid foundation, rather than becoming yet another new media company that bursts onto the scene, only to fade away soon after. I was aware of the bleak statistics: 90 percent of startups fail. I knew that given our momentum, Mogul could be poised to be part of the 10 percent that succeed. I also knew I had spent every day since I made a vow to follow in my grandmother's footsteps preparing myself for this very moment. I had the skill set to make this work. But I had a long road ahead of me. I would need to bring on investors in order to keep our momentum going, and to ensure that our rapid growth did not lessen. Handling every aspect of Mogul from my bedroom was not a long-term strategy, especially once we reached one million women, so I would need to build a team to help in this endeavor.

This can be the scariest part for some people. When you have to trust your idea, get up in front of people, and pitch who you are and what you are doing. When you have to let go of controlling every aspect of your concept and bring on partners to further your growth and expansion. But understanding that you can't go it alone is a key moment in every dreamer's growth. By listening to your gut and truly believing in what you are doing, you'll find that with the right people by your side, you can go farther than you ever imagined.

ALWAYS RECIPROCATE

I've learned time and time again that opportunities often come down to the people you know, and how much they are willing to put their necks out for you. As I've stressed before, it does not matter what degree you have or what school you went to. People are the ones who get things done, who will connect you to the very person or very company that can change your life. And the only way you find people willing to do that is if you are good to them. This is the path of reciprocity, and it can be a major accelerator. You never know how the next person you meet might be able to open doors for you. **So always be kind, be generous, and be willing to go the extra mile.** When they do that in return, it could be the very opportunity you've been looking for.

I first met Alex through the director of *Girlfriend,* who was one of his close friends at the time. He'd heard about how I delivered on the distribution side for *Girlfriend,* and that I was working at CBS, and we soon struck up a friendship. Alex had just launched a startup that did digital distribution, and he invited me to join his company's advisors. It was the first time I'd been approached to be an advisor to a technology startup, despite years serving on various nonprofit boards, and I wasn't quite sure what it would entail, but I liked Alex and felt like he would be a great collaborator, so I signed on. I soon found myself on monthly phone calls with him and the other members of the team, and it became clear that an introduction to CBS would be beneficial. I was more than happy to connect him with a colleague, though I had no direct say. Alex landed CBS as a client shortly thereafter.

It was just a few months later that I began coding the first version of Mogul. When Alex heard about it, he insisted on introducing me to a few of his other advisors and friends. So just a few weeks after Mogul launched, Alex sent off about ten emails. "Will, you have to meet Tiffany. She just launched a company, she's one of *Forbes*'s '30 Under 30,' you have to see what she's doing and get on board." Okay, that's not verbatim, but you understand the passion with which he wrote these emails, and the urgent sense he instilled in their recipients that this was someone you wanted to pay attention to and a company you didn't want to miss.

As a result, I soon found out that Will, a cofounder of Match.com, wanted to set up a call.

Now, I had known that bringing on investors was the next step for the company. But I was so busy keeping the site going that I hadn't yet taken the time to create a pitch deck. Our phone call was scheduled for the next day, so I quickly threw something together, practiced my pitch in front of my parents and brother, and then tried to take some deep breaths.

The next afternoon, there I sat, on my bed in my apartment, when the phone rang. It was time for my first major pitch. I nervously answered and started talking about Mogul. About its trajectory. All the numbers and where I envisioned the company going. Once I got started talking about Mogul, the nervousness subsided somewhat. The passion I felt about Mogul and the impact it was already having took over. But as I wrapped up the pitch, I knew this was where I had to nail the ask. My brother had suggested a line for the end of my pitch: "I would love to invite you on board as an investor."

I thought it was a great way to end my pitch. But I tweaked it slightly:

"I would love to invite you on board as both an advisor and investor."

Pause.

"Yes, I'd love to. Can you send me the documents today?"

My heart stopped. He just said yes! Now what?

I just really hadn't thought it would be a yes. As a result, I hadn't thought about what I should say next. My silence stretched uncomfortably.

So, then, I brilliantly said, "Oh, what documents?"

I heard a soft chuckle. "Next time, before you talk to someone like me, you should go to YCombinator.com and download the SAFE note agreement. And also, go to the Founder Institute website and find their standard advisory agreement."

I laughed (to match his laugh, no pun intended, though I was also kicking myself) and thanked him in advance for his support and collaboration. He said he would get me on a call with his investment partners shortly, as a formality.

I shuffled out of my bedroom, still a bit stunned, where my parents and David were watching TV, something I had not been able to do for months.

"He said yes!" I said with a huge smile.

My family cheered, so happy and proud. They enveloped me in a hug. All the sacrifice, all the late nights, had led to this moment.

The next week I got on the phone with the partners of Will's fund to discuss the details of the company, and they finalized their investment then and there.

I had my first investor and advisor. And it was the cofounder of Match.com.

That never would have happened without Alex, who appreciated me helping him with his company and now vice versa. When you support others in their endeavors, and when you treat everyone with kindness, generosity, and respect, it will always come back to you, oftentimes when you least expect it.

Avoid These Mistakes When Pitching

Throughout your career, there may be times when you need to pitch an idea, or sell a new initiative internally, even if you are not an entrepreneur. The company for which you work may have asked you to develop a new product and pitch it internally to receive buy-in and funding from senior management, for example.

As a result, I wanted to share with you some of the mistakes I've made in presenting, so you can be sure to avoid the same ones. Though I nowadays generally "pitch" over tea and conversation without the use of a pitch deck, in the early days of Mogul, I always used a pitch deck in order to visually convince someone to come on board, sharing slide by slide our mission and metrics.

When I pitched Will, I didn't know that I made some pretty major mistakes:

1. The background was black. Which looks great on a screen. But if the person you are sending your presentation to prints it out, it is hard to read, plus you owe them twenty-five dollars for new toner for their printer. Most likely, they won't even want to print it out. So don't make your presentation on black, no matter how powerful that may look on a screen.

2. Because I was so data-focused from my HBS background, I put all the most impressive data on one slide, resulting in a very crowded and hard-to-read slide, instead of spreading it out and giving each data point space on its own. What I know now is that each slide should be making a point—hitting a home run on its own—otherwise, it's not needed. In other words, if this slide was the only slide that someone saw, it alone should make him or her believe in what you are pitching. Not because it is filled with

data, but because it packs a serious punch and makes a point all on its own.

3. The logos I used were too small to really see. If you have a logo slide of partners or other investors or backers or clients, further establishing your validity, blow up those logos. In the end, every small "yes" you get will help you land a bigger "yes." Therefore, collect and display those small "yeses" proudly; use them to create more momentum.

Luckily, I didn't know how bad my deck was when I went into my call with Will. Ignorance is bliss, right? But I quickly made sure to fix it before going to my next investor meeting.

FOSTERING FOMO (FEAR OF MISSING OUT)

Getting that first yes was a huge accomplishment, not just for my confidence, but because I truly believe that one yes will lead to the next yes, which can lead to a snowball of yeses that eventually grows into an avalanche of yeses.

Though I'm not sure I would ever advise someone to have their very first pitch meeting be with one of the top veterans in their industry like Will.

But I wasn't going to say no to that opportunity, and, in many ways, I believe that the fact that Will was involved from the very start, that he gave me those nuggets about where to find information about a SAFE note and an advisory agreement, led to even more emotional investment in me and the company.

As I went on to pitch additional investors and potential advisors,

I soon learned one of the most important elements was what Alex had done for me in the very beginning. With his initial email, he created this fear of missing out in each of his contacts.

Now, while you may be familiar with that phrase in terms of sitting at home, watching your friends' social media feeds, and feeling completely left out, Fear of Missing Out in the venture world is something a little different. Creating FOMO in an investor means they are more likely to invest because they don't want this potential unicorn to pass them by. You make them want to be the one who saw the seeds of greatness early on and didn't miss the boat.

It is a powerful tool to use.

Creating fear of missing out requires a delicate balance. You don't want to oversell what you are doing, but you want to approach people with the sense that you are going to be hugely successful with or without them. That you are headed places and they can get on board and enjoy the success, or walk away and realize later what a great opportunity they passed up. This is applicable whether you are building your own company or working for someone else. By talking about what you are doing and what is happening in your company with passion and conviction, it makes the listener realize that they will absolutely miss the boat if they don't join the team, buy your product, attend your conference, or whatever you are asking of them.

Talk It Up

Even before I officially launched Mogul, I was talking about it with everyone I knew. Please don't make the mistake of keeping your idea to yourself. You have to talk about it. With everyone. Your best friends, your family, the person on the subway next to you, the person in the board meeting. Why? For one, it helps you hone your pitch. You'll quickly develop your elevator pitch once you go on for too long and see people's eyes glaze over. You'll determine what point about your project makes people light up with excitement. You'll discover what follow-up questions they have, and those questions will allow you to further refine your product.

I soon established a pattern with each of my pitches. I focused on two things: 1) the storyline of momentum, detailing the lifelong passion and unending dedication that led me to Mogul. And 2) the numbers, showcasing the traction that we had already received so that no investor could ever say this platform was not needed. At the time that I pitched Will, we were reaching one million women across 130 countries. I gave him access to our analytics so he could see for himself. The numbers were able to prove to investors not just the potential that was within this company, but the fact that there was a proven audience for this site, and they were hungry for its content and community.

One of the reasons that I built Mogul before pursuing seed money is I was aware of the fact that men are often backed for the potential of their companies, while women have to prove they can deliver. I knew that I had three strikes against me going into these meetings: 1) I'm a female. When I started Mogul, less than 10 percent of all startups had a female founder. Men were 60 percent more likely to get funding than women. In fact, of the $50.8 billion that venture capital firms invested from 2011 to 2013, just $1.5 billion (or 3 percent) went to companies with a woman CEO. 2) I'm a minority. The only other group more passed over than women is minorities (83 percent of venture-backed companies consist of founders who are entirely Caucasian). 3) Mogul was in the media sector, one of the most competitive spaces in venture. The fact that I had already built a platform reaching a million people allowed me to showcase the demand. I was able to show the numbers and stand firm on this being a needed product because the metrics validated it.

But I had one more secret weapon—I had coded the platform myself. Even if investors were on the fence about the opportunity, that fact pushed them over the edge. To them, it showed that I was different; I was fully invested in this company, and I was willing to get involved in every single aspect of it.

Consequently, no one wanted to miss the chance to partner with us.

Never underestimate the power of passion to persuade people of what you are doing. Show people how completely invested you are, whether pitching your own company or trying to spread the word about someone else's. Live, breathe, and believe in your product. Others will follow.

MAKE THE PROFESSIONAL MORE PERSONAL

There was one more thing about my pitch that made me stand out. The story of Mogul was personal. At the end of the day, venture capitalists don't invest in products; they invest in stories and people. It's important to give them a reason to care. Of course I shared the personal story of my family and how they were my inspiration, but I also made sure to share the stories of the women reaching out to me and what access to information, opportunities, and education could do for women across the globe.

Whenever I pitched Mogul, most of the people in the room were men. Just 4 percent of venture capitalists are women. But I didn't let that change my personal story or how I communicated our mission. I focused on how Mogul was becoming a platform for all women, a way for women from all walks of life and cultures to come together and support each other, ultimately being able to accomplish together way more than they could have on their own. This storyline connects all of us. Mogul was not a company that was solely focused on a business plan but on a mission, and a mission is always personal. It is always about people. Yes, my goal was to make money for investors, but my personal goal was to take the profits that Mogul generated and use them for further social impact. The end goal was not money. It was impact.

Being personal has always served me well. And it extends outside of the boardroom. I do not believe that your personal life and professional life have to be completely separated. In fact, I think having that perspective is detrimental to your career trajectory. First of all, my colleagues inevitably become my friends. Again, I don't believe in networking; I believe in finding like-minded individuals with whom you can truly collaborate. Collaboration isn't a business relationship. It is a creative partnership. It is a meeting of the minds that allows each of you to build off of the other's idea. This allows you to create something that never could have been realized alone. With this kind of collaboration, you ultimately build a friendship based on the foundation of trust that you develop over time. Soon a conversation over business problems can morph into a conversation on relationship problems, or issues at home. When you trust someone in one area of life, it is natural to begin to trust him or her in other areas as well.

When you learn how to comfortably mesh who you are professionally with who you are in your personal life, you are allowed to be the most authentic version of yourself. And that is your best self, always. We had a young team member at Mogul who had just graduated from college. And she was very "church and state" when it came to her professional and personal life—in other words, keeping them separate. When she met clients outside work it was all work, no play. But I knew that in her personal life, she was very funny and relaxed. I had seen that side of her several times, and I knew that if she revealed that aspect of her personality with her clients, she would win them over even more. When you are who you truly are at all times, in all situations, it allows other people to see your true self, and what you, and only you, bring to the world. It is contagious, attractive, and refreshing. Always.

I've heard it said that Albert Einstein is one of the most famous scientists in the world not just because he was the best in his field, but because he was funny and memorable in addition to being brilliant. He was truly himself, which led him to become one of the most recognized scientists to this day.

When you bring your personal into your professional, it allows people to connect with you more readily. Let me give you an example. Shortly after Mogul was launched, we were awarded the 2014 IVY Innovator Award, and I was invited to L.A. to receive the award and speak briefly about the founding of Mogul. The reception was to take place at a film premiere at the Landmark Theatre. I had arrived at my hotel and planned to work on my speech when S reached out, asking if I could come pick up some stuff that I had left at his apartment. It was just a few months after our breakup. I told him I was in L.A., and he seemed annoyed. Because of that, I couldn't concentrate on writing my speech.

When I arrived at the theater, I had no speech in hand. And it turned out that the publicists present wanted me to escort the star of the film, Daniel Radcliffe, down the red carpet. I was shocked and honored to be Harry Potter's date for the evening, but was like a deer in the headlights as paparazzi immediately swarmed in front of us, shouting and taking photos of us hugging (you can only imagine what S thought after that).

As we headed up the stairs after the red carpet, to wait backstage for when they would announce the award, I saw one of my business school classmates. "Chrissie!" I shouted, shocked to see someone I knew from Boston out in L.A. We caught up on what we had been doing since graduation, and I saw her hesitate a bit before she shared, "Actually, I just broke up with someone about a month ago, and I'm still kind of getting back on my feet." I listened to her story and couldn't get over the parallels to my story with S. When she finished talking, I said, "Oh, Chrissie, I just went through the exact same thing." And told her the story of both Mogul and S.

We had not been close at HBS, no more than acquaintances. But because of Chrissie's willingness to be open with me, we connected on a really deep level. She is now one of my dearest friends because we took the time to relate personally and support each other.

When I walked out to accept the award, I saw her out in the audience, beaming with kindness and support. I still had no speech written, but seeing Chrissie spurred me on and reminded me of how strong we both were. A wave of calm set in, and as I stood before several hundred people hanging on my every word, I told my personal story of Mogul, the promises I had kept, the personal sacrifices I had made, the long nights we had seen, our vision just ahead. I spoke with passion and conviction, knowing that it was much more powerful because I had brought all of me into the story of Mogul, my personal commitments and sacrifices as well as our mission and goals. The audience exploded with applause.

How to Be Personal in a Professional Setting

Obviously it is not always an appropriate time to share your story about a recent breakup. But too often I've seen people hold back aspects of themselves that could serve them in their professional lives. And when connecting with potential collaborators, sometimes it is your shared personal experiences that can really bond you, allowing for a much closer relationship than you ever would have had if you kept something to yourself. So if you are in a setting where you are one-on-one with someone, or in a small group, if you are out to dinner or at a social event, take the time to consider whether this might be a chance for you to go a bit deeper and share something personal that you would never think to share in a board meeting or visiting them in their offices. Doing so could be an accelerator for your relationship, leading to more trust and more collaboration down the road.

REMEMBER TO STRETCH

To be successful, you have to trust that you have what it takes to accomplish any goal and allow yourself to aim high and reach far. One of my favorite investors has always been Gary Vaynerchuk. I had been a fan of his ever since he was vlogging about wine back in the early 2000s and grew his family's wine business from three million to sixty million dollars. Since that time, he has become a true hit maker, becoming an early investor in companies like Facebook, Snapchat, and Twitter. Of course I wanted him to join Mogul. To have him on board would truly be a dream come true, and a signifier that Mogul was garnering widespread support.

I had previously met the founders of MakersKit at Techstars and had written about them and their company for *Forbes*. Months later, after launching Mogul, I discovered that Gary was an investor in their company, and though I didn't think it likely that they would agree, I reached out to see if they might be willing to put me in contact with him.

And they said yes! The path of reciprocity came through yet again. Before I knew it, they had connected me with Gary and his right-hand man, Phil Toronto, via email. I met with Phil in front of Shake Shack in Madison Square Park. He talked about their fund, only further convincing me that they would be perfect investing partners, as I talked to him about Mogul.

About a week later, it was time to pitch Gary himself. I was sitting nervously in the conference room with Phil when Gary walked in. I stood up and introduced myself and then launched into my pitch, about one minute in, Gary said, "I know Mogul is a winner. You're a winner. I'm in."

I was stunned. He had literally been in the room for not more than a minute. I didn't know what to do, and so I tried to continue with my pitch. Just in case he needed further convincing. Gary laughed and made it clear he didn't need to hear it. Phil had already filled him in, and he liked what he had heard within the first minute of my pitch. He wanted to be a part of it. The entire meeting lasted less than ten minutes.

I walked out of there completely shocked and elated, and I had to confirm with Phil several times that that had really meant a yes.

To achieve success and significance, you have to go after those stretch opportunities. I didn't think the MakersKit team would say yes when I asked them to introduce me to Gary. I didn't think Gary would immediately say yes when I pitched him, but I didn't let that stop or discourage me. **It pays to believe that with all your hard work, the best scenario could happen.**

It often does.

Later, after we achieved significant momentum in our funding, I was able to establish certain standards when I met with potential investors. No phone numbers were exchanged. No meetings were held in hotels or bars. Instead, I invited them for tea between the hours of 3:00 p.m. and 5:00 p.m. at our Mogul headquarters, which was advantageous because then they would be able to meet the team and see how passionate we were. This enabled me to also go into these meetings from a position of strength and know that investors who took the time to come to our offices were really excited about the possibility of investing.

Finding Investors

Ideally, when reaching out to a potential investor in your company, you should use a warm connection. If you are just starting out in your fund-raising endeavors, you can go on LinkedIn as a first step and search for "Angel Investor" within people's titles. Then, review what kind of companies they invest in to ensure they are interested in your space. Next, look to see whether you have any mutual connections listed. If so, reach out to that mutual connection to see if they might facilitate a meeting. Angel investors will sometimes invest in a company after just one or two meetings and often have connections to the venture capital world that you wouldn't have otherwise. As an investor once wisely told me: "You beg, beg, and beg the angels. Then, once you've gotten yeses and significant dollars have been committed, that's when you go to VCs."

BUILD A TEAM YOU CAN TRUST

While I was pursuing investors, I was also working to expand the team at Mogul. Given our growth, I knew that the idea of me working alone in my bedroom for two or three years was not realistic. Although I loved being a part of every single aspect of Mogul, I would be holding it back if I didn't enlist others to come join me and help.

Mogul truly started as a family endeavor. It was built in my two-bedroom apartment that I shared with my brother. David may be three years younger than me, but as mentioned, he was the tech prodigy in our family and a highly sought-after technology leader in New York City. So when the platform would sometimes crash in its first few weeks, given all the users, he would quickly get it back up and running. Most websites have a team of engineers on board by the time they reach one million people. That wasn't the case for us, and I'm not sure where Mogul would be if David hadn't stepped in when our users and I needed him.

An incredible brother and mentor, David was a constant source of support and a sounding board during those first few months, while Mogul continued to scale.

At this time, as a serial entrepreneur with several successful books and ventures under his belt, David had been considering founding his next startup. But as he watched Mogul thrive at levels that we never could have anticipated, it was clear to all of us that he was already a part of the team, stepping in daily to lead the platform through these viral levels. We never even had a conversation about it. David was one of our founders, and is now our brilliant chief product officer and chief technology officer.

Some people say they can't work with family, but David and I have always had a close relationship. We don't recall ever even having a fight throughout our lives, to this day. One of the most beloved members of our team, David has a calm, wise, philosophical manner that others adore, and that commands great respect across all the divisions and team members within Mogul. And with that, we are able to communicate with just a few words, which is pretty handy when you are in important meetings and someone throws a curveball. We are always on the same page, and I trust him implicitly. He so deeply believes in our mission, in what we are doing. He's exactly the kind of exceptionally brilliant person you want on your team.

Then, about three months after Mogul's launch, I met Namisha, a graduate student in marketing at NYU, originally from India, who was interested in an internship at Mogul. We agreed to meet for an interview at Argo Tea in Columbus Circle (since I was still otherwise working from my bed). I was twenty-seven years old, and when Namisha walked in, I was convinced that she was in her thirties: her experience was extensive; she had raised millions of dollars for various organizations; and she spoke with a level of maturity and confidence that superseded my own. In fact, she had offers to join multiple well-established companies. But against the warnings of her professors, she, too, believed in Mogul's mission deeply, and wanted to join our team over the others. I felt confident that she would be a great partner, and we very much needed the additional support in these months while Mogul was exploding.

I offered her the opportunity on the spot.

What I soon learned was that Namisha is not afraid to share what is on her mind. From the get-go, she always seemed to have a differing opinion from everyone else. In those early days, when I was still developing my skills as a manager, I found her perspective challenging to counter, and I sometimes felt trepidation to bring something up. But I soon found that her pattern of disagreeing with something I proposed about 90 percent of the time led us to really hash out each issue, think about the pros and cons, and engage in important debate that ultimately led us to the right path forward each time. I'm not sure where Mogul would be if I hadn't had Namisha there every step of the way, questioning our decisions and pushing us to think through every project and opportunity. She was never afraid to add her voice to the mix.

It wasn't until a year and a half after we'd started working together that I actually learned Namisha's age. The day she walked into Argo Tea? She was just twenty-four years old. The bottom line is, it didn't matter how old she was. What mattered was what she brought to the table, the perspective she wasn't afraid to share, and the way she was able to dig into our work and truly be a powerful debate partner.

She knew Mogul as well as I did, even better at times. Namisha is now VP of global marketing and Mogul Redefined, our consumer products division.

And then came Bethany, from Texas. I first met her thanks to Rob.

About a year after my working with him, he came up to me and said he had someone he wanted me to meet. "I have a prophecy that the two of you are going to work together. That you'll be business partners one day."

By this time, I trusted Rob and his opinions deeply and couldn't wait to hear whom he wanted me to meet. At the time, Bethany was getting an MFA at Juilliard; I was getting my MBA at Harvard; and Rob felt that the combination of Bethany's creative expertise from Juilliard and my business acumen from Harvard would be the perfect meshing of talents.

We met for tea one cold afternoon at Au Bon Pain in Union Square, and right from the start, I could tell we would become good friends. We were both beginning to get our feet in the door in the film industry, and Bethany showcased herself to be someone who was determined and went after what she wanted. At the time, for example, she was performing in a production of *The Merchant of Venice* starring Al Pacino. She had hustled to get that role.

Bethany asked me to accompany her to an event for her friend Anna, an up-and-coming screenwriter, that very week. When we arrived, we learned that Anna was dating a man named Sam, Rob's lyricist on *Volleygirls*. We then realized that Monica, the producer of *Volleygirls*, had gone to Juilliard with Bethany, and they had been friends since. Our worlds were highly connected, and that was the first of many industry events that we began to attend together, where our friendships and relationships continued to exponentially grow and deepen. Together, we were offered more meetings and more opportunities, and meeting each other proved an important accelerator in both our personal and professional lives. Rob's prophecy was right.

Therefore, Bethany was one of the first calls I made when launching Mogul. And today, she is our VP of global content and Mogul Studios, our creative agency and content production division.

As Bethany came on board, we began to meet at the Hudson Hotel, two blocks away from Argo Tea. We joked that we were very slowly expanding the perimeter in which we needed to travel. We met each morning inside the Library Bar of the hotel, stationing ourselves at one of their large chess tables for a full day and night of work ahead. And even though we weren't hotel guests, we hoped we were paying the staff back in a way with all of the Diet Cokes we ordered throughout those following two months.

One afternoon, about six months after launching Mogul, I was walking back home from "the office" and I saw an advertisement for a new work space called the Yard, located one block away from my apartment, where ABC News used to be. I met with the owner, Morris, and immediately signed the lease for one of their offices, which, ironically enough, was called the Library. I'll never forget that moment when we first moved from the Library Bar to the Library. As I looked around the room, I grasped the fact that our company now had an office and team members—a small and mighty team of four: David, Namisha, Bethany, and me. It had grown from a dream in my mind, to a reality in my bedroom, and now into an actual company. Even as I'd made all those pitches and received all those investments, this was the moment when it truly felt tangible. In the months that followed, we continued to expand throughout the Yard, securing additional space for our office more than six times as we added new team members and became one of their largest tenants.

Interestingly, my relationship with S brought me one of my closest friends to this day and the next founding team member of Mogul. I even remember as I was saying goodbye to S, remarking: "I'll really miss hanging out with Juli."

Juli's former husband was one of S's best friends from Princeton. S and I had hung out with the two of them on three separate occasions, one of which was their wedding. It was therefore strange for me to instinctively say I would miss Juli, because at this point, I still hardly knew her. And out of all of S's friends, we had hung out with them the least.

But two months went by, and I did not hear from any of S's friends except for, coincidentally, Juli. She reached out because she had come to love Mogul. She was on our platform every day, starting conversations, as was her sister. They had become super-users.

At a serendipitous lunch over sushi one day, Juli asserted her ongoing passion and dedication to the Mogul mission and offered to help in any way. Without hesitation, I offered to bring her on part-time. I developed with her what would initially be a small but vital role, mainly focused on editing, but Juli assured me she was up for anything.

She wasn't kidding. Even though she had led operations and customer support at different companies across Hungary by the time she was twenty-four, now, years later, she was willing to do anything and everything to help our company grow. I soon learned that if we needed something done, she would immediately teach herself. If we needed video editing, she would teach herself Final Cut Pro. If we needed photos, she became an expert at Photoshop. She would teach herself totally new software just so that she could help us in the next task. She rolled her sleeves up, and would over-deliver on every single project. She was the definition of a mogul.

Within a few months, she joined us full-time. Today, she is our VP of global operations and people, overseeing our infrastructure globally.

This founding team has truly been with me from the very beginning. I didn't cross my fingers and hope they were "good hires." These were people whom I greatly respected, who had proven themselves to me over and over through many months, sometimes years, of collaboration, stepping up whenever something needed to be done. I had no worries that if I had to travel to meet with an investor or potential partner, they would be able to keep things running. Each of our founding team members represents a different part of me, from David's unending calm and wisdom, to Namisha's determination and persistent questions, to Bethany's emotional intelligence and relationships, to Juli's hustle and motivation for continuous improvement.

I cannot stress enough how important it is to have the right people surrounding you as you go after your dream. **Your company or concept can become even greater if it is in the hands of the right team.**

Be Mutual in Your Commitments

From the beginning at Mogul, when I first hired people, I would bring them on as consultants for one to three months before committing to a full-time contract. This allowed everyone to ensure that it was a good fit, and that we meshed well as a team, before a long-term commitment was made.

Obviously not all industries can work this way, but if there is a way to ask for a trial period before you commit to something full-time, it both allows your employer to make sure that they are happy and shows that you are someone who, when hired full-time, is truly loyal and committed. It shows thoughtfulness, a cautious but committed attitude, and a willingness to check in constantly to make sure that everyone is happy, fulfilled, and communicating about expectations and experiences.

REMEMBER A "NO" IS A "NOT RIGHT NOW"

But of course no matter how loyal your team or how strong your relationships, the best scenario doesn't *always* happen. To become a mogul, you have to be prepared to hear the word "no." It is inevitable, no matter what you are going after. But the word "no" doesn't have to be a fail. First of all, you should be reaching out to so many people—many of whom will say yes—that the one or two little "nos" don't sting. You stay focused on the "yes." When you have reached out to a huge volume of people, you forget the "no" and move on.

Another helpful thing to consider is that the "no" is just a "not right now."

Just a few months into Mogul's founding, a startup accelerator reached out to us to see whether we would want to apply to be a part of their program. Startup accelerators are organizations that help startups quickly grow so that they are in a stronger position to go after investor funding. In return for granting a small sum of capital, and access to some of their contacts, accelerators usually get a small stake in the company. But they can be very selective in who they take on.

We appreciated that this accelerator wanted to consider Mogul, so we went through the application process, the rounds of interviews, and made it to the finals. For the final round, our team walked into this big room, filled with about twenty people (only two of whom were female). David and I gave our pitch and then allowed the room to experience the platform themselves as they scrolled through the site. Everyone seemed impressed and positive until one person said: "Um, what's that?"

We looked up at the screen and, in the time that we had been giving our pitch, a user had posted a link to a *National Enquirer* article about a mermaid sighting.

Yes, a mermaid sighting.

Bethany was also in the room. She and I looked at each other. Before we developed proprietary technology to prevent spam in real time, Bethany and I would regularly scan the new posts on the platform, in order to make sure that this kind of spam didn't turn up. When she or I caught such posts, we would remove them. But because our entire team at the time was sitting right there in that room during this pitch, obviously no one was monitoring incoming posts.

Our positive pitch had now turned into a grilling session. As we walked out of the room, we knew that what would have been a "yes" had turned into a rejection, all because of that mermaid sighting. When we got the email a week later that we didn't get chosen, none of us were surprised.

But we didn't find it devastating. We had a lot of momentum even without this accelerator, and we stayed focused on the "yeses" we were getting. Within a matter of months, we had secured funding not just from Will and Gary, but also from the founders of Comcast and TheKnot.com as well as the heads of MTV, *Fortune*, *Time*, NPR, McGraw-Hill Education, Diane von Furstenberg, and the Hearst Corporation. Our snowball was turning into an avalanche of "yeses" just as we'd predicted. It turned out that our relationships and friendships, and the excitement that Mogul was generating on its own, were our own kind of accelerator.

A year later, out of nowhere, this same accelerator had been tracking our growth and reached out and wanted to invite us to join them. We wouldn't even have to apply; we would automatically be in. They felt like we were the company that got away. But by then, we'd grown much larger and faster than any of their other investments. We didn't need to be a part of their accelerator anymore.

The lesson is, when you receive a "no," just keep moving forward. **There will come a day when those who initially said "no" to you will come chasing after you, in disbelief at your success.** (Just ask J. K. Rowling if you need additional proof—she's said that twelve publishers rejected *Harry Potter* before one took a chance on her.)

One of the reasons that I'm good at dealing with "nos" is that I tend to forget all the "nos" right away. I joke that I have a bad short-term memory for "nos." I look forward, not back, and just move on to the next opportunity. Because at least I learned something, remember? Sometimes these "nos" are the best things to happen to you. Those opportunities would have been detours on the path to success that you didn't need to take. Allow those exits to pass by without remorse. Trust that you are headed in the right direction and that more opportunities lie before you.

ESTABLISH YOUR OWN BOARD OF ADVISORS

The next step for Mogul was to establish the Mogul Board of Advisors, a sounding board and governing body that would allow Mogul to become greater than just our small but mighty team at the time. Advisors would also add another layer of validity and expertise to Mogul, and become a rich source of advice when making important decisions. When I envisioned our ideal board of advisors, I thought about every aspect of a media and technology business, such as finance, operations, content, marketing, product, and technology, and tried to think of the one person in the industry that I respected the most in each segment. I then approached that person to be an advisor.

As mentioned, I first invited Will, cofounder of Match.com, as an advisor and investor, given his experience in scaling online platforms. Michael Wolfson, cofounder of TheKnot.com and former chief creative officer at AOL, came on board next, given his insights on content creation and distribution. I then invited Cathie Black, former chairman and president of Hearst Magazines, for her expertise in creating iconic brands, as well as Ann Sarnoff, president of BBC Worldwide Americas and member of the Board of Directors at PayPal, for her experience in overseeing finance and operations for organizations worldwide. They were soon joined by Jarrod Dicker, CEO of Po.et Foundation and former head of product and technology at *The Washington Post*, whose rapid product innovations had fueled the latter's growth post–Amazon acquisition;

James Benedict, founding advisor to the crown princess of Norway's Maverick Collective, for his contributions toward global social impact; as well as Kevin O'Donohue, former managing partner at BC Partners and Stanford University philanthropist, and Peter Davis, former president of McGraw-Hill Education, for their significant contributions to education. The final board member added was Tina Exarhos, chief content officer for NowThis Media and former chief marketing officer of MTV, for her pioneering experience in viral marketing.

This required another layer of pitching, with a slightly different approach. I still kept it very personal, mentioning how invaluable I would consider their involvement. And I often traveled to their offices for the meeting, wanting to emphasize that I knew we would be collaborating closely if they joined this board.

Every time a new advisor came on board, it would offer one more layer of opportunity, validity, and proof that Mogul was a company that countless people were getting behind. Soon we had so much momentum from talking about Mogul and what it was doing that we created a second advisory board called the Mogul Think Tank, a more informal group of advisors who were such believers in our platform that they wanted to offer their help and expertise as well. Our Think Tank today consists of twenty-five women and men who believe greatly in our mission and have been partners in our growth. I can come to the various members depending on what kind of advice I am looking for or what kind of partner Mogul is currently in need of.

Finally, we created a network of Mogul Influencers, prominent women and men such as Katie Couric, Nina García, Rebecca Minkoff, Margaret Cho, and more, who were on the Mogul platform and who vowed to spread the word about what we were doing to their own followings. Today, we collaborate with more than five thousand Mogul Influencers, who mentor our users, befriend them, and support them.

You may not be launching your own company and in need of an

official board of advisors, but I nonetheless recommend a personal network of support to help you navigate your career path. Your personal board of advisors could be former managers with whom you've stayed in touch, favorite teachers or professors, and even good friends who you know want the best for you in any and all endeavors. You may consider your mother and father to be an essential support system, or your brother and sister. We can accomplish so much more when we feel that we have people to turn to for advice or just as a sounding board. We can do more, be more, and reach our goals sooner. Together, we can break down any barrier that still stands in our way.

Learn to Just Ask

It is never easy to gather the courage to ask someone to be a part of what you are doing, but you never know what he or she might say unless you ask. I remember when I asked Anne Hidalgo, the mayor of Paris, to be a Mogul Influencer. She and her advisors had selected Mogul, along with a few other startups, as a top New York City company, and thus awarded us an office location in Paris as well as other resources, to facilitate our expansion in France. She invited me and the other founders to meet with her and other members of her cabinet.

The Mogul team had already drafted a physical letter to ask her to join our Mogul Influencers, and I held it in my lap during the entire session. As we were preparing to leave, I struggled with finding the courage to go up to her and hand her the letter, especially in front of so many others present.

But I knew if I didn't, I would always regret it and wonder what she would have said.

As the meeting wrapped up, I took a deep breath, gathered my confidence, walked up to her, and said: "Actually, I have a letter for you. I would love to invite you to be a Mogul Influencer." And I explained to her what it was.

She looked at me warmly, smiled, and said, "Absolutely."

It was that easy!

The worst that could happen is that they say no, and you move on. Either way, you'll always feel better knowing that you tried. That one moment of rejection is a lot shorter and less painful than the years of regret you might feel for not asking.

It is the greatest feeling to have a broad basis of support. **When you have others who are supporting you, you no longer feel like you are alone in the driver's seat.** Now you have passengers able to provide input and advice when needed. Not to mention these people came with their own network of relationships and ideas that will allow your reach to expand even more. What is truly amazing is being able to join with the right people on the journey, people who will spur you to become better and stronger and aim higher and farther. When you have the right people by your side, you become poised to launch into the next stratosphere.

#YouAreAMogul

To strive for success means you have to be able to communicate who you are, why you are the one for the job, and why people should join you in your endeavor. Make them realize how much they will be missing if they don't join you. In the end, have the confidence to know that you are going places with or without them.

#IAmAMogul

By Simone De La Rue, founder of Body By Simone and celebrity trainer on *Revenge Body*

The success of Body By Simone has surpassed even my expectations. Sometimes I look around and can't believe what the business has evolved into. I was a professional dancer for eighteen years, and that was my first true love. I watched some of my younger colleagues taken down by injuries early in their careers and knew I had a set of techniques that had kept me injury-free over the years.

I wanted to create a place where women could come to feel strong and sexy, where they could come to connect with their bodies and themselves. I initially started with a small number of loyal celebrity clients, who were thrilled with the results and spread the word. After a client, who appreciated and believed in my vision, invested $100,000, the business grew from personal training to forty employees, tens of thousands of devotees, and studios in both New York and Los Angeles.

I never anticipated how rapidly the company would grow. Having not gone to college, I relied on my intuition and curious mind-set to drive business decisions. **It proved essential to take each step carefully, be highly reactive to clients' feedback, and build the company piece by piece, decision by decision.** It didn't happen overnight, but our loyal clients' endorsements helped to create rapid growth in the business early on.

Staying true to my intuition and vision for the company was incredibly important to me. I even took the risk of buying out an initial partner to allow the business to continue organic growth in a specific direction.

I know now that it was thanks to being true to who I am and my vision for Body By Simone that allowed it to take off and reach more people than I ever imagined. I don't feel like I have reinvented the wheel; it's just exercise, right? But the fact that I get to help women across the country focus on their health and believe that they deserve to take the time to feel good and connect with their body is the greatest compensation I could ever ask for.

8 RIDE THE ROCKET SHIP

Mogul is frequently portrayed in the media as a rocket ship, though you've since learned, of course, how hard we had to work to get there. We are often asked: *How did you rise so far so fast?*

I believe it has been thanks to a commitment to stay true to ourselves, remain focused on our vision, and ultimately, to always circle back to our mission, or why we built Mogul in the first place.

We didn't do everything perfectly. But we stayed focused on what we were doing and, more important, why we were doing it. Rather than thinking about the long road before us, we took it step-by-step, opportunity by opportunity, always remembering that we were the ones in the driver's seat. When you think like an entrepreneur, you see each and every moment as a chance to accelerate, to grow faster than you ever thought possible. And you have to keep moving forward, no matter what.

These are the guidelines I used for growth, trusting my gut, and always knowing we were heading in the right direction. I hope they can help you and your career to take off quickly, and go farther than you ever imagined.

THE 3 C'S: COMMUNICATION, COLLABORATION, & CELEBRATION

As we began to scale beyond our initial team members, we moved our headquarters to Hearst Tower at Columbus Circle (next door to Argo Tea and the Hudson Hotel). We were right back where we started, only now with a library of our own and a view of Central Park.

We realized we had a real opportunity to create the kind of workplace culture that is too often missing in the corporate world. The culture that we've created today has most definitely contributed to our incredible growth. I really do not believe we would have achieved what we have without it. And as a result of our creating this culture, not one single person resigned from Mogul for the first four years.

Okay, I'm sure as this book goes to print someone will quit, thus nullifying that statement. I probably shouldn't even put it in the book, since it is something that is bound to happen over time, as we are expected to triple in size this year.

But this is something that I am proud of thus far, and I like to think that it has to do with the culture at Mogul that we've worked really hard to cultivate. A culture of kindness, compassion, and understanding. A culture where we don't have to keep personal lives separate, where we strive to create friendships, not just colleagues. You can bring all of yourself into the Mogul offices, not just part of who you are. This focus has led not only to happy team members but to the growth that has kept Mogul going.

Just as women make up 80 percent of our platform, women also make up 80 percent of our leadership team. We provide unlimited vacation, unlimited sick days, and unlimited remote days. Because when you trust your team members, you don't worry about them abusing those privileges. I know that each and every person who works at Mogul loves her or his job and believes in the mission, and if they need to take some time off to recharge, we trust them. If they are too sick to come into the office, we trust them. If they believe they will be more efficient accomplishing something from home, we trust them. And they trust us, that we have their backs. We provide strong health benefits and subsidize gym memberships. We provide free dinners and free cars back home for anyone still at the office after 10:00 p.m., to ensure safety. We regularly issue raises and bonuses throughout the year for reaching goals, without waiting for annual reviews, through a cutting-edge system we developed called the Mogul Individual Performance System, or MIPS. The system has been highly tailored to each team member in order to help guide and support them across each aspect of their role, and in turn reward them.

The benefits of having team members who feel valued and supported far outweigh the costs that these perks carry.

We also regularly consider each team member's personal passions that they might have otherwise conducted as a side hustle, and we aim to incorporate these as added responsibilities in their professional day-to-day role. Again, if you had to keep your personal and professional lives separate, I wouldn't know that you happen to be a skilled photographer in your off-hours, or that you often MC at the comedy club down the street. These skills can be incorporated into your job at Mogul, allowing for further acceleration of your career. We strive to nurture our team members' talents and encourage them in all aspects of their lives.

Melinda Gates wrote that we are still "sending our daughters into companies designed for our dads." We are thankful that isn't the case with Mogul. Mogul was built to support women around the world externally, through an all-inclusive culture internally. It isn't afraid to challenge the status quo for what a startup should look like or how a leader should act. **The more of us who are willing to do this, to demand a workplace culture that respects women and their way of working in the world, the quicker we will rise, the more female leaders will come into power, and the more authentic we will all feel in our careers.**

There are three values that set us apart in our office culture, and that I strive to keep in mind as I focus on what Mogul should be. I call them the three C's: communication, collaboration, and celebration.

Communication: We believe in absolute transparency and real-time feedback in our offices. My door is always open, and I encourage our team members to come to me about anything. If you feel like you have to hide what is truly going on with you at work, you can't truly be your authentic self. I believe that when you can bring all of who you are into the workplace, you will be able to do your best work. When you bring your entire, authentic self to work each day, you can thrive personally and professionally; this lack of hindrance enables creativity and new ideas to emerge that greatly serve the company.

Throughout the day, I'm constantly walking around the offices talking to people. *What more can I do to support you today? How are things going?* I strive to stay involved in the day-in-day-out of the functioning of Mogul. I don't want to be sequestered in an office on my computer or in meetings all day. I want to be accessible, available, and supportive all day, every day.

If we've brought someone onto the Mogul team, it is because we value the insights he or she brings to the table. So when I'm in a meeting, and each of the executive team members has shared their thoughts, and I see someone at the table who is more junior who hasn't spoken up, I try to encourage them to join the conversation. "Lauren, you always have a useful perspective. What do you think?" Usually that little nudge, combined with something complimentary, will give them the courage to speak up. And I've often found that they respond with the most eloquent solutions that they had already come up with in their head but just hadn't had the nerve to share.

As a leader, you want to ensure that every voice is heard. You want to nurture the talent that you have brought into the

workplace. You want to encourage ideas, out-of-the-box thinking, and the willingness to think of a new perspective.

Admit to Mistakes

One tool I have used when discussing feedback with a team member is if a miscommunication occurred, and a lack of management may have contributed to this miscommunication, I'm always up-front about that, and I apologize for whatever mistake was made. I find that being up-front about how management might have been unclear leads the conversation to go more smoothly, because it eliminates any defensiveness your team member might have that would prevent them from even hearing what you are saying. By addressing that issue up front, you accelerate your way to a solution.

This works both ways. To get a conversation off to a great start, you, too, may want to admit to how you might have contributed to a problem, so as to immediately move into problem-solving mode. Your coworkers will appreciate your willingness to admit to fallibility and will be more likely to want to collaborate again.

Collaboration: Obviously, by now, you know I believe in collaboration. I believe that two minds coming together, bringing their various experiences and perspectives into one room, is the most powerfully creative thing in the world. I have worked in organizations that were hierarchical, where there was a clear delineation between the supervisors and the worker bees. I was so appreciative when someone higher on the totem pole would bring me under their wing, allow me into meetings, and give me experiences that taught me so much and allowed me to collaborate with them. But those people were the exception, not the rule. At Mogul, whether you are a senior leader or a direct report, everyone collaborates as equals, as partners.

Another way we strive to stay collaborative is by never eating alone. Each meal can be an opportunity to connect with someone new, and create further collaborations and synergies across projects and initiatives. Every day I take a different team member out for breakfast or lunch, to connect with them on both a personal and professional level; and everyone else is encouraged to do the same. Beyond meals, we have weekly meetings so that we can stay aware of where people need support. On Mondays, I meet with our executive team. On Wednesdays, I meet with every department, back to back, in forty-five-minute time slots. This midweek check-in allows us to refocus on goals, any new opportunities, and our mission. Once a month, we have a Monday town hall when everyone in the company gets together to collaborate on our most challenging initiatives.

We also have regular lunch-and-learn sessions where different departments take turns sharing their expertise or industry insights with the remaining departments, again to increase potential for collaboration as every team member enhances their learning. Mogul also provides annual reimbursement for coursework a team member wishes to take online or in person for this purpose. If a team member hopes to incorporate these newfound skills into their role, we highly encourage it and find a feasible way to do so, in order to continuously weave team members' personal passions into their day-to-day roles and ensure everyone feels personally and professionally fulfilled.

Celebration: At Mogul, we work hard, and we celebrate when things go well. When you look for the good, you find more comes your way. We therefore share wins in real time across the company, via an internal Mogul channel called #wins. From morning to night, anyone who has a win can post an announcement that allows the rest of the company to cheer along with that person. This creates ongoing minute-by-minute momentum and high morale throughout the day and week.

By the time we reach Friday evening, before everyone departs for the weekend, we celebrate our Weekly Wins. Each member of the company shares what went well that week, whether it is a milestone achieved, a new account or client, a goal set and accomplished, or a creative idea they are most proud of from that week. This not only allows our team members to feel a sense of accomplishment, but lets the different departments of our company recognize how we are all part of a whole, and how essential each department is to our success. We don't just celebrate professional wins either; quite frequently, team members will use their moment to share to instead highlight another team member and commend a selfless action they had secretly noticed from the week, an interaction they deemed to be kind, authentic, and generous. This atmosphere of constant celebration and success just breeds more celebration and success. And having such a positive meeting at the end of the week means people go into the weekend encouraged and excited about the next week to come. Especially when we toast, using the fourth "C"—champagne.

Celebration continues throughout each month and quarter, thanks to the efforts of our Mogul "Turnt Club," a cross-department committee formed to strengthen our team bonds. They help us celebrate birthdays and organize team outings, including our annual retreat to a city of significance to Mogul, as voted on by the company. Each June, we also celebrate our anniversary, which in recent years has included unlimited shopping sprees at Barnes & Noble to encourage continued reading and learning. Finally, for team members who celebrate five years at Mogul, they may fly to any library of their choice in the world, as a nod to Mogul's historical journey from the Library Bar to the Library and our continued social impact on education worldwide.

I know that staying focused on these three C's has helped our culture stay consistent and has helped us focus on how to lead our team in the best way possible. When you have these touchstones, you can refocus over and over, making sure you stay on track.

What Are Your Touchstones?

When you think about the kind of company you want to run, or the kind of company you want to work for, what values come to mind? If you could list three things that are most important to you when you are looking for a culture fit for a workplace, what would they be?

1. _____

2. _____

3. _____

Culture fit is extremely important in your overall happiness at work. There are times when, no matter what the job looks like on paper, if the culture doesn't fit with your values and what encourages the best work out of you, you are going to feel a mismatch. Just like in a dating relationship, not everyone is going to be a perfect fit, and we can sometimes waste the best years of our lives at a place that isn't building us up but is sucking us dry. While experience is important, to feel 100 percent valued and fulfilled at work, you've got to find a place that is a cultural fit as well.

DISCOVER WHAT TRAITS BREED SUCCESS

One way to know whether someone or someplace is a cultural fit for you is to determine what traits you value the most in an employer or team member. Do you value ambition and the hustler mentality? Do you value a collaborative spirit or creative thinking? Do you value dedication to the task, someone who will stick with a problem and work at it until it is solved? All of these are valuable traits that will be most of service to different people and various industries.

I've learned that for me, I look for people who are kind, authentic, and generous, willing to collaborate, and who love to learn. And also someone who is dedicated not just to making money, but to making a difference. Those traits were always foremost in my mind when it soon became time to add additional members to Mogul beyond our founding team.

I also ensured that I had someone in charge of human resources very early on. As Juli became full-time, she soon assumed the role of head of HR when it came time to add additional team members. It is highly unusual for a startup to have a head of HR as team member number four, but I knew that creating the right culture and hiring the right people was just as important as finding the right investors and building momentum.

Our hiring process today has four rounds. The first round involves direct sourcing, resume reviews, and an initial phone interview between the candidate and the hiring manager or an HR team member. The second round involves inviting the candidate to do an assignment, through which they can showcase their talent and passion for Mogul. The third round involves an in-person meeting with both the hiring manager and an HR team member. The hiring manager is looking for raw talent: someone who is smart, sharp, and willing to go the extra mile. Our HR team member is focused on culture fit: Are they kind, authentic, and generous?

Are they here for the mission? Do they love to learn? At this point, if our hiring manager and HR team member think this could be a good fit, then the third round also involves in-person conversations with David and me. David and I know Mogul equally well, and together, our further assessments confirm the candidate's skill as well as cultural fit. We provide one additional layer of screening for the kinds of people that make Mogul a coveted place to work. If we observe any hint of meanness or misogyny, the candidate is eliminated. If they seem inflexible and unwilling to evolve with the growth of the company, we know they won't be a fit. We look for the kind of passion and compassion that comes from being mission-oriented. That, to us, is a sign they are right for this place.

Finally, the fourth round involves time spent with the wider team. Past this point, the job is theirs. We bring them into whatever department they would be joining and have them spend a few hours with the team. This final round just confirms that they are the right fit for us, and that we are the right fit for them.

It is a lengthy process. But I know that it has served us well and has led to our incredible retention rate. **The people you invite onto your team will lead to the success or failure of your dream.** They are the people you will be surrounded by each day. The people who will reflect on you or your company in meetings, in message boards, everywhere they go. You want to make sure that you select the right people. Take time to figure out a process that is right for you and stick to it. Trust your gut. If there are any red flags, listen to them, heed them, and wait for the right person to come along to fill the role.

This goes for when you are interviewing for a job as well. You want to ensure that it is a cultural fit for you, just as much as you want to impress them and show your talents. Do the people in the office seem like the kind of people you want to surround yourself with? Is there a spirit of collaboration, which will allow you to put your "intrapreneurial" mindset to work? Does the person whom you will report to possess the skills you are looking to develop? This is ultimately why you should authentically be yourself throughout the interview process, to ensure it's a true mutual fit for the team and for you.

Secrets to Nailing the Interview

Research the company beforehand. Become aware of any new deals, mergers, or important milestones reached. Follow them on social media, so you'll be aware of anything new that arises, even on the day of your interview.

Clean up your digital presence. Download the Social Sweepster app, which will flag pictures of suspicious objects or any posts with profanity.

Schedule it right. Try to schedule your interview for Tuesday at 10:30 a.m. Okay, it doesn't have to be so precise, but when you have your interview is important. You want to avoid Monday or Friday, when the interviewer may be distracted, and you don't want an interview right before lunch, when an interviewer may be hungry. Obviously you want to work with their schedule, but the earlier in the day, the better, so that they have a chance to think about you and refer to you in conversations with others. Ultimately, it helps them to remember you, which is key when there is a lot of competition.

Remember your storyline. Take a moment to review the storyline you are featuring with your resume and application. Have a few stories already prepared that you can work into any question they ask of you. Make sure to stay focused on PAR—what was the **P**roblem you addressed, what **A**ction did you take to solve it, and what was the **R**esult, or what changed thanks to your action?

START SMALL TO SUSTAIN YOURSELF

Establishing a team that you can trust is essential to your business success. But at the end of the day, you've got to be able to pay their salaries. You must discover a way to monetize sustainably. I never wanted Mogul to be dependent on financing. I wanted it to be a company that earned its own revenue. It began early on with selling marketing campaigns on the site. This was an easy way to stay focused on making the platform as strong as possible, engage with our users, but still have some revenue coming in. But we knew that we wanted Mogul to be more than just a platform; we wanted it to turn a profit so that we could take that profit and invest it into other areas, leading to even greater impact.

Any time we considered growing in a new direction, we stayed focused on two things. 1) Does it align with our mission to empower women across the globe with access to information, opportunities, and education? If the answer was no, that wasn't the right direction for us. 2) Is it scalable? In other words, can it grow indefinitely, reaching more and more people, providing more and more revenue, and more areas for Mogul to expand, with continued efficiency? If the answer was yes to both of those questions, it was worth exploring.

The very first revenue-generating division at Mogul was called Mogul Studios. Taking Bethany's and my background in content production and distribution and Namisha's expertise in marketing, we planned to partner with different companies to help them authentically connect and engage with women on our platform and channels, through marketing campaigns. We had access to millions of the very customers many brands hoped to reach. This would enable us to impact and influence the ways in which companies were communicating with women, externally.

Step one: we knew what we were trying to do. But we had to get to step two: acquire some actual clients.

We were brand-new in this space and didn't have any success stories to prove our worth and skill. So initially, I had to beg people to partner with us. Yes, you read that right. In the early days of Mogul, I begged people to partner with us. You can't have an ego when you are an entrepreneur. You've got to ask over and over and over again, for a warm connection, for a lead, for a job. I reached out to several fellow female founders and pleaded with them to trust us with a campaign. Did they have marketing dollars in their budget? Did they need to reach new customers? We had a fast-growing network and we promised to deliver.

People did not say yes right away. We were still new, after all.

Once Soraya agreed to our first campaign at $500, our next client, located in Singapore, invited us to pitch three times before she said yes. But she ultimately agreed: we could produce a campaign consisting of twenty pieces of written content for her. For $2,000. In a month's time.

This was not a great deal. In fact, this was a very difficult deal to execute. **But when you are just starting out, listen carefully to what your first clients are requesting and make a few initial deals, even if the terms are lower than what you would like in the future.** It gives you a chance to succeed and prove your worth. Then you have a case study to show the next potential client. And step-by-step, you will work your way toward being able to charge what you know you are actually worth.

That month was painful. It takes a lot of work to create one piece of content for a campaign. And now, we had to create *twenty* pieces of content, in a very short amount of time, for what felt like next to nothing for our bank account. But we did it; and the client loved our work and was extremely happy with the results. Now, we had a case study to show the next client, who partnered with us to spearhead a campaign for a new brand that was targeted at women. This time, we were paid $5,000 for one piece of content. Another case study for our portfolio. Our next deal was for $35,000, for our first major corporate partner, who had grown interested in Mogul due to our case studies. And with that, our fees continued to increase, along with our client base. Soon, Mogul Studios was partnering with hundreds of companies, and within three years, companies were offering between $1 million and $10 million per campaign. Time and time again, we pitched alongside Facebook, LinkedIn, and other giants, in order to win these marketing campaigns. Today, we partner with Fortune 1000 companies worldwide.

As an increasing number of companies began coming to us with different kinds of content to create and distribute, we also began to partner with TV networks, studios, researchers, and publishers who would reach out to create content in collaboration with us. Women's voices and perspectives are grossly underrepresented in the media. Only 15 percent of feature films feature a female protagonist. Male speaking parts in films outnumber female speaking parts three to one. Thus, Mogul Studios today is additionally coproducing and collaborating on Emmy-nominated shows and feature films, publishing research and books, and more, all focused on reshaping storytelling for women and ensuring it is empowering to women worldwide.

But it didn't start there. It started with twenty pieces of content for $2,000.

So no matter where you start, remember you are riding a rocket ship. Where you start is not where you'll end up. You've just got to start somewhere, believe in what you are doing, and go after what you want.

Tricks and Tools for Getting a Response

When selling, it takes on average six tries to get a response. So you can't stop after two or three tries. You must be tenacious. This applies to reaching out to potential mentors as well.

At Mogul, we use a couple of different software products that help us do business. One is Rapportive, a tool that will ensure that you are using the correct email address. It helps even further by giving you the person's complete background when you hover over their email address, allowing you to tailor your request or pitch.

We also use Streak software, which allows you to know if someone has read your email or not, and on what device and in what location. This allows you to see, for example, if someone is traveling at the time, and so they probably didn't have a chance to read your email in full.

Sometimes having this additional information gives you the confidence to reach back out several times to ensure you eventually get a response.

FIND THE RIGHT PERSON

Sometimes the growth of your company stems from coming in contact with the right person at just the right time. This happened to me, and it led to the creation of Mogul's second division, Mogul Redefined, as well as the final member of our founding team. My former colleague Scott (the one who had been the first to text me about *Forbes*'s "30 Under 30") had recently reached out, wondering if I could meet his younger sister, Natasha. He thought it would be a mutually beneficial meeting, but he additionally hoped I would become a mentor to her. As we met for tea, I found Natasha to be razor-sharp and worldly, given her French and German background, yet also kind and soft-spoken. Having graduated magna cum laude from Georgetown, she was currently working at an education foundation, developing case study materials for Columbia Business School and Parsons School of Design.

About nine months after I launched Mogul, she asked to get together again. She passionately asked me if there was anything she could do for Mogul, either part-time or free. She really loved what she already knew of the organization, had been an active user on Mogul since its inception, and was hopeful for the opportunity to collaborate.

At that time, unfortunately, there were no opportunities open at Mogul. Our team was so small, after all, just David, Bethany, Namisha, Juli, and me. But I loved her initiative in coming forward with this request. It reminded me of all the times I had done the same. And I was also impressed by her remarkable ability to persuade, given her otherwise gentle demeanor.

The next morning, I woke up and had a sudden vision for exactly what Natasha could do at Mogul. That very week I had happened to create a road map for Mogul to develop educational courses that would enable women to continue their personal and professional development. These courses, I envisioned, would cover topics across every facet of a woman's life.

Was it aligned with our mission? Absolutely. Was it scalable? Of course. We could offer these courses to our users across the globe.

And Natasha had just the right experience to execute and lead the way.

So I called Natasha up, pitched her the idea behind Mogul Learning, and said that while we didn't have a full-time position at the time, we would love to bring her on part-time. Our intention would be that this would morph into a full-time position within about six months.

She said yes and jumped in immediately. Together, we eventually created award-winning courses composed of more than 1,200 course modules, ranging from becoming an entrepreneur, to rising to the top of your chosen profession, to personal finance, higher education, relationships, engineering, health and fitness, and more.

Mogul Learning launched in October 2015 with a huge event hosted by Natasha and our friends at WeWork. The feedback we received was incredible and inspiring, as our users thanked us for providing them the kind of personal and professional guidance and development they had been asking for since Mogul's inception.

Mogul Learning has ultimately become one of the core products offered by our consumer products division, Mogul Redefined. Mogul Redefined is redefining what it is to be a mogul by developing innovative and cutting-edge education-related products for our users, just as we did with our platform.

As for Natasha, we celebrated her transition to full-time at the launch. And today, she is VP of global sales and Mogul At Work, the next division at Mogul to reveal itself to us.

KEEP YOUR EYES OPEN FOR WHAT MIGHT COME NEXT

Just like meeting with Natasha prompted the creation of Mogul Learning, it is important to always be open to where your company might be wanting to grow. Look for signs that it is the right time for expansion. Sometimes we have set ideas for what we want to accomplish but we don't know the exact timing. By being flexible yet strategic, you stay focused on what you want to eventually accomplish but allow the correct timing to reveal itself.

Shortly after Mogul Learning launched, we began reaching millions more women per week. Our platform was growing fast and companies realized that there was an immense network of driven, ambitious, intelligent women convening on Mogul every day. Natasha and I were sitting in a meeting with the Estée Lauder Companies one day when they asked a question that more and more companies had been asking: Could they have an employer profile on Mogul so that they could post jobs to the community and access the top female talent that made up our user base directly?

I had always intended that we would build out in this way, to essentially move into being the very platform where women would look for a job. That Mogul could not only be the platform where you went to share meaningful conversations, with real questions and real advice, but also be the space where you actually connected with your next opportunity. But I had been persuaded by others to hold off. Wait until the demand was there; wait until companies came to us to ask for this privilege. Now we couldn't ignore that there seemed to be true demand.

The Estée Lauder executive left the room briefly, and I was pacing back and forth. This was it, Natasha and I decided. We needed to start this new division. Give these companies that were already working with us through Mogul Studios for marketing the ability to create company profiles on the site for HR. This was an additional way to monetize as well as support our mission. There would be an annual subscription fee to have a profile. So it was scalable. And giving our users direct access to job postings was definitely in line with our mission. Natasha and I couldn't wait to wrap up this meeting so we could get back to the office and start hashing out the details of this new software.

Mogul At Work was soon born, the third revenue-generating division within our organization. Companies are able to talk about their mission, their culture, their values, and more, so that women are able to understand what kind of company they are interviewing for. They post job openings across the world, helping us accelerate the rate at which women are obtaining managerial positions and above (currently, women represent only 10 to 20 percent of top leadership positions). Within just a few short months of launching this new software, we had more than a hundred company profiles. Today, we partner with Fortune 1000 companies worldwide and communicate with more than twenty thousand HR departments, including, of course, the Estée Lauder Companies.

Mogul At Work has since expanded to offer a full suite of HR software to companies, advancing diversity and inclusion in the workplace. Such software includes company webinars to train employees and overcome challenges like unconscious bias. This enables us to impact and influence the ways in which companies are communicating with women internally.

As I'd seen in my time at Harvard, unconscious bias was a real hindrance for women across all industries, but there weren't any strong programs to help people overcome these biases. Companies were on their own to provide any kind of workshop, and while some human resources departments were proactive, most were reactive at best. I knew that one of the ways to increase opportunities for women was to tackle some of the internal issues they faced that had nothing to do with their qualifications and everything to do with inherent biases in hiring managers and CEOs across all different industries. These webinars would be a way for Mogul to address many of the issues that women face in their career journey: lack of promotions, lower wages, and lack of women on boards. By providing trainings on unconscious bias, inclusive leadership, and gender equity to Fortune 1000 companies and more, like the New York City Department of Education, we might close the gap that has been eluding us for years.

I have no doubt that Mogul will continue developing many new innovations and cutting-edge technologies and products to help women worldwide. But Mogul has been the story of building slowly but surely, and allowing the company to tell us when it is time for more growth or a new division. As Sheryl Sandberg once said about Mogul, we did it by "following our customers and following where they grow."

Sometimes we have so many ideas in our head for what our company could do, it is hard to know where to prioritize. It can be hard to pace yourself when you know where you want to go and grow. **But I encourage you to be patient and watchful, always ready to take a leap, but never leap without knowing that it is the right next step for you.** It can be tempting to say yes to every offer that comes your way. But by creating benchmarks that allow you to stay focused on what you created your company for, you can stay focused on what partnerships and growth are really right for your company.

#YouAreAMogul

Your dream may flame out if you don't take steps to carefully ensure its ongoing success. Trust your gut, be patient with your growth, and choose very carefully those you entrust with your mission. But when you do this, you won't be on a roller coaster. You'll be riding a rocket ship.

#IAmAMogul

By Katrina Lake, founder and CEO of Stitch Fix, and youngest founder and CEO to take a company public

I love apparel retail—it's a large, meaningful industry in which people are thoughtfully buying things that they will love for years and years, things that represent who they are.

I realized early in my career that I loved the industry but I didn't know immediately what company to join or what role might suit me. I just wanted to be part of a team that was creating the future of retail, and I saw that future as a more personal, convenient, relevant, and fun way to help people find the things they love. My own personal experience influenced my conviction. I think many people can relate to wanting to feel great and confident in their clothes but find themselves prioritizing the most important things in their lives and not having time to shop. Neither traditional retail stores nor spending hours searching e-commerce sites seemed like a great solution, and I knew there had to be a better way.

Initially, I flirted with the idea of joining a retailer, but ultimately felt that it was going to be too hard for existing retailers to boldly change and that disruption would most likely come from elsewhere. I joined a venture fund, hoping that I'd have the chance to meet a team that shared my vision for the future. I met over a hundred entrepreneurs coming in to pitch their ideas. Many were inspiring and bold, but most of all, I realized they were just as inexperienced as I was. There didn't seem to be an exact profile of the "best" background for an entrepreneur. All were armed very simply with a deep belief in themselves and their company—and I realized that I could do that, too.

I started Stitch Fix while I was at Harvard Business School to tackle a very human problem: **How do I find clothes I love, and that fit me, and help me to feel my best?** The idea of making personal styling scalable and accessible was one that got a lot of engagement and excitement from the women I knew, even before we had a website or even a business plan. It was also a concept that I could test relatively easily with online surveys, apparel from local boutiques, and many friends and friends of friends. I was able to quickly gain confidence that it was a strong value proposition for women everywhere.

Building this business into a successful enterprise was going to require capital and support. I was introduced to Steve Anderson, one of the first investors in Instagram and Twitter, by a mentor of mine. Steve believed in me and my vision, and in early 2011 made a commitment to invest $500,000 in the company. I was thrilled to be officially off to the races, and to get a chance to work with Steve, an incredible and experienced partner for me and for Stitch Fix.

Less than a year later, Stitch Fix had a handful of employees in downtown San Francisco. Every Monday, it was all hands on deck getting Fixes out the door, and we resumed our day jobs for the rest of the week. Our client base grew through word-of-mouth referrals, to people all over the country, amplified by bloggers and influencers, both large and small.

It was clear from the feedback and the organic growth of our client base that the business had real promise, and it was important to build an incredible team to help bring it to life and realize its potential. While it might have seemed like a disadvantage that I didn't come from a big, well-known company with a large network of established connections, I actually found that it provided me with freedom. I looked at LinkedIn and at my school alumni network websites as a yellow pages of sorts, and found it inspiring and empowering that I had so many amazing people within reach.

Two of my first leadership hires—our COO, Mike Smith, and our chief algorithms officer, Eric Colson—are still with us today. Mike was the COO of Walmart.com before he came to Stitch Fix in 2012. He was looking for a startup company to join that had a unique and disruptive approach, and where he could be really hands-on with the teams. In fact, before he even started at Stitch Fix, Mike came to help the team pack Fixes on one of those "manic Mondays," he was so passionate about the business. Eric was the VP of data science and engineering at Netflix before he joined our team. Initially, Eric was an advisor to the company and was constantly tinkering with the incredible amount of data we had amassed in a short period of time. He was so intellectually attracted to our bold model of shipping recommended items directly to your home that he joined full-time to build a data science team from scratch. All of our early employees shared the same passion for Stitch Fix's mission, had the vision to see its potential to scale, and possessed the grit we needed to make it work. Just as important, they believed in me and my vision, and this empowered me more and gave me the confidence to continue pursuing my dream.

This "Stitch Fix Grit" has been critical to our success as a business. Even with our seed round in hand, and one of Silicon Valley's top investors committed to the business, the process of raising more funds for Stitch Fix was difficult. After Steve's initial round we met many more investors, but despite having a great team, a real and growing business, and clients who loved us, we still couldn't get any new investors passionate and excited enough to invest in the company.

After many months of little progress on the investor front, in late 2012, we found ourselves with less than eight weeks of cash left. In the decision to become an entrepreneur, I had contemplated and was comfortable with the risk involved; I was okay living in a small rental apartment, driving an old car with windows that didn't go all the way up, and eating instant ramen. I hadn't fully contemplated what it would feel like to be in such a precarious position and to have employees who were relying on me. Mike and Eric, for example, had given up careers at big companies to take a bet on Stitch Fix. They had mortgages and kids in school. The sense of responsibility was enormous and not something I was prepared for. Steve Anderson and I got together and worked through the Excel spreadsheet that was our finances and our business plan. Together, we figured out how we could get to cash flow positive, less reliant on investors, and have more control over our destiny. It was a difficult time but also an empowering one; with a plan and a small bridge round in place, we were on a clear path to making Stitch Fix profitable and self-sufficient.

Today, Stitch Fix is a billion-dollar business with over 2.4 million clients. We have incredibly strong product market fit, and a practical but also deeply emotional value to millions of clients that we serve every day. Seven years in, we're only just at the beginning of understanding what we can learn, and how we can grow.

Viewing the world through a wide lens of possibility is one of the greatest gifts. **To be able to imagine something that's never been done, to achieve the seemingly impossible, to be able to believe in something that few others can even comprehend—this is the magic and essence of what makes entrepreneurship possible.**

9 MAKE THE MOST OF EVERY DAY

Being a mogul is not about building a company, securing investors, or heading an office full of employees. Being a mogul is about pushing every day to find new opportunities for growth, whether personal or professional, always being on the lookout for ways you could achieve greater impact or partner with a new collaborator. It means setting yourself up, each day, to be ready for what comes.

I believe that small acts can totally transform your life and that the routine you establish for your days can lay the groundwork for success or failure. So I wanted to share how a typical day goes for me, and some tools that I've learned to use to make the most of each hour of the day. Now, typical is not really typical. My days change all the time depending on if I am traveling or what kind of event I am going to. But this is how I set myself up for success, how I stay energized throughout the day, how I stay focused on what I am doing and what I need to accomplish, and how I stay inspired to keep at it and wake up excited the next morning.

A DAY IN THE LIFE

Before I go to sleep. Visualize. My day actually starts the night before. Before I head to bed each night, I review my calendar for the day ahead and hour-by-hour **visualize** how I can over-deliver based on the goals of each conversation and meeting. What is the one thing that I need to happen in each meeting for it to be rendered a success? I visualize that happening. Visualization is something I learned to do early on in my life. I find it to be a very effective focusing tool, and it helps me identify what I truly need to make each interaction as powerful as it can be. Then, I am ready to sleep, confident that I know my goals for the next day.

Wake up early. I usually don't set an alarm, and instead let my body naturally awaken, usually around 6:30 a.m. Even if I do set an alarm, I **never hit snooze**. As much as you may want to squeeze in five more minutes of sleep, resist the urge and get up immediately. You want to feel yourself spring up from bed, feeling inspired for the day ahead. Even one push of the snooze button may set you up for a day of being late or procrastinating what you need to do. And five more minutes of sleep are likely going to make you feel drowsier, not more rested.

Exercise. In order to provide myself with as much headspace as possible to think about the day ahead and what I must accomplish, I stick to a morning routine so I don't have to expend any extra energy on what I need to do to get ready. I start the day by training each morning at a nearby dance studio called Body By Simone. I find this is the most likely time for me to be able to squeeze exercise in. If I wait until after I leave the office, I may have an evening event to attend or a dinner. So I throw on my workout outfit, grab my phone so I can listen to some energy-inducing music on the way to the studio, and get my body moving, first thing in the morning. I have so much fun dancing. The exercise puts me in such a bright and happy mood for the rest of the day.

Dress. I select an outfit the night before to ensure that I have the perfect look ready to match what I have to do during the most significant moment of that day, whether I am taping a TV segment for *Good Morning America* as soon as the morning hits, giving a speech at the United Nations, or meeting with our team of advisors. I also suggest that you establish a unique uniform for how you dress. This not only helps with indecision about what to wear, but it also creates a look that people associate with you. For me, I wear black dresses. When it is cold in New York, I wear black tights and black trench coats over them. But I pretty much always have on a different variation of a black dress. Think about Jenna Lyons or Anna Wintour or Nina García. They have a look that everyone associates with them. Establishing your unique uniform ensures that you leave the house every morning feeling your best and like yourself. There's nothing worse than buying trendy pieces of clothing and feeling like you are putting on a costume, instead of being comfortably who you are. You want to feel confident, classic, and totally you throughout the day. This starts with what you put on each morning.

Connect. Every day, fifteen of my closest girlfriends around the world text me good morning and vice versa. We check in with each other as a way to feel connected and supported no matter how busy life gets. Then I check my inbox and **prioritize which emails to respond to first**. In any given hour, I can receive hundreds of messages, ranging from questions from Mogul executives to emails from partners to special requests from users. This triggers me to focus on the places where I most need to optimize. What is most likely to move the needle for Mogul in this moment? Whatever the answer is, that is the email I prioritize next.

Breakfast. I head to the first meeting of the day. I often have breakfast meetings at the same café near the dance studio before I go into Mogul's offices, which allows me to both refuel with a healthy meal and strengthen my relationship with whomever I am meeting. Sometimes it is with a team member from Mogul, other times it is with a fellow entrepreneur. We share some personal stories, some professional stories. This is usually not a task-oriented meal but a meal focused on connection and friendship. I strongly believe that everyone has something to teach, knows something better than you do. Therefore, I usually aim to uncover what that topic is over the course of the meal, and delight in learning what they know. This allows me to go into the day feeling most like myself when I've connected with someone deeply.

Head to Mogul HQ. I usually arrive at the office by 9:30 a.m. I sit at the opposite end of the floor from the entrance doors. Therefore, I must walk through the entire HQ before I can make it to my desk. As I pass by, I check in with each division and each team member, seeing if and how I can support them today and if any needs arose that morning that I haven't already addressed by email. Sometimes, I may not actually make it to my desk until one or two hours later! Otherwise, I soon have back-to-back meetings with division heads, investors, advisors, partners, or reporters. I ensure that we end each meeting deciding the exact next step; whether a document needs to be sent or a follow-up meeting needs to be scheduled, it gets done that day.

Lunch. At Mogul, we love catering lunch for the whole company, and it's a great way to continuously strengthen team morale. It's important to make sure you take the time to eat lunch—no matter how busy the day gets. I believe in never eating lunch alone, so if I'm not eating with the entire team, I use this time to eat with a different team member each day and continue to build our friendship.

Collaborate. I make it a goal to have at least one meeting per day in which I'm meeting someone new—someone who's innovating in their own space, someone who might jolt an idea in you that will help move the business forward. I also try to schedule most of my meetings in the afternoon, after lunch, when my energy starts to lower. I invite guests to Mogul HQ and have a lounge area set up with tea and snacks so that it encourages a warmer and more personal connection. I schedule the teas for thirty to forty-five minutes. Placing these meetings back-to-back in the same location keeps my mind clear before and after, freeing me from the pressure of travel times and directions. This allows me to stay energized as I meet each new person and stay focused throughout the day. I do meet outside Mogul HQ as well, but on those occasions, I have admittedly been found sprinting across avenues with Namisha in heels, in order to make meetings on time (because cars in New York City are often slower). We pretend like we didn't just run a marathon once we arrive.

Dinnertime. After a busy day of meetings, I usually refuel around 6:00 p.m., while I catch up on email for the day and respond to various phone calls and texts that have remained unanswered. I often order food in, using one of the many food delivery apps that have made our lives so much easier! I love you, Seamless, Postmates, and Caviar.

Social event. In the evenings I often have events to go to, or a chance to see something that a friend is involved in, whether it is a charity event or an art gallery opening. These events are great opportunities to reconnect with people I love, talk about what Mogul is doing, and meet potential new collaborators.

Home. I'm usually back home around 9:00 p.m. This is when I unwind for the day, change into pajamas, and then usually hop back onto my computer for more work. I aim every night to get to inbox zero.

Check in on the next day. After midnight, I wrap up work for the day and start to assess the day ahead and align goals for tomorrow. Before heading to sleep, I like to reflect on the events of the day to potentially change my perspective and see things in a different light, which then enables me to present concepts and tasks to my teams in continuously improving formats. Think about situations you could've handled differently or times you could've communicated better. As mentioned, I take this time to visualize success for the next day.

Sleep. Once visualization is complete, I'm very serious about optimizing my sleep conditions. With the few hours per night you rest as an entrepreneur, you must maximize your bedroom surroundings to the best of your ability. First, disconnect from your electronic devices. The bright screen on your phone or laptop can badly affect your ability to get a solid night's rest. Ensure blinds or curtains are fully closed to create the best sleeping environment. Try listening to calm music or an audiobook. Personally, I turn my phone on Do Not Disturb. Continue to get much-needed sleep and rest, no matter where you are in the world.

That's a broad overview—here is one specific day I had recently, to give you a snapshot.

6:00 a.m.:	Wake up.
7:00 a.m.:	Dance studio.
9:00 a.m.:	Skype into Puerto Rico to speak with our users.
9:30 a.m.:	Arrive at Mogul HQ. Meet with executive team.
10:00 a.m.:	Chief diversity officer for Bank of America.
11:00 a.m.:	Chief people officer for the Honest Company.
12:00–3:00 p.m.:	Video shoot at the Broome Hotel.
12:30 p.m.:	Catered lunch for Mogul team at HQ.
1:30 p.m.:	Call with United Nations, UNICEF team.

2:00 p.m.:	Head of talent development at Stanley Black & Decker.
2:30 p.m.:	New product review meeting.
3:00 p.m.:	UK investor meeting.
3:30 p.m.:	Head of talent for Flatiron Health.
4:00 p.m.:	Catch up with singer-songwriter Kari Kimmel.
4:30 p.m.:	Chief marketing officer for Revlon.
5:00 p.m.:	Reporter for *Glamour* and *Teen Vogue*.
5:30 p.m.:	Champagne toast, celebrating wins with our team.
6:00 p.m.:	Head of employer branding for T-Mobile.
6:30 p.m.:	Catch-up emails with CMO of General Mills, CMO of Mercer, and CMO of IBM North America.
7:00 p.m.:	Reporters for *Inc.* and *Forbes*.
8:00 p.m.:	Birthday dinner.
12:00 a.m.:	Work on this book but try to sleep soon. (I've gotten better about this over the years.)

ROLL WITH THE PUNCHES

So that's a typical day for me, more or less. But because of the nature of running a startup, no day is ever the same. Sometimes I'll start a day thinking it will look one way and it ends up looking completely different. As much as you might plan things out thoroughly, you have to allow for spontaneity.

This past fall, for example, I was invited to be the keynote speaker for the International Day of the Girl Child hosted in Paris. After my talk, I flew back to New York, went straight to Mogul HQ, and had ten deals with Fortune 1000 companies to close across all of our divisions. That night, the Mogul Studios team was headed to Boston to host Chelsea

Clinton and former U.S. Secretary of State Madeleine Albright for our #AskAMogul series. There was so much studio equipment necessary that we didn't have enough people headed to Boston to take it to Penn Station, so I hopped in an Uber with the team to help transport it. On the way to Penn Station, we learned our Uber driver was from Boston, and when we joked that he could just drive us straight to his hometown, he replied he would be up for it. Soon enough, we were all headed to Boston together for the next five to six hours, myself included. All I had were the clothes on my back, no toothbrush, no pajamas, no change of clothes. I hadn't planned on going with the Mogul Studios team. But I changed plans on the fly. I picked up a toothbrush and some pajamas at Walgreens when we got to Boston, and I spent the next two days alongside Madeleine Albright and Chelsea Clinton (at least once in my new pajamas).

In the end, what does remain the same for me is that every day is about high impact. It's important to perform at 100 percent in every moment—with true kindness, authenticity, and generosity.

DEALING WITH STRESS

I've often heard from friends and colleagues that I am the "chillest hardworking person" they know. And I think that's because I strive to be fully present wherever I am. During the course of the day, I try not to think about what I am doing next, or what meeting I was just in, when I need to be in the now. I try to stay focused on who is in front of me at the moment.

I had a speech teacher in high school mention that when she met a former U.S. president, he made her feel like she was the only person in the room. He made her feel like she was the most interesting person there. Somehow that always stuck with me. I wanted to make people feel that way as well. As mentioned, I've come to approach every conversation as an opportunity to learn; after all, everyone has something to teach, something they know better than anyone else. Seize this opportunity to uncover what it is. It helps you connect with people on a deeper level, and it also keeps you focused on the now. It keeps you from stressing about what you need to do or what you just did. You just see what is in front of you. And then you move on to the next thing.

Throughout my life, whenever I've felt the tendency to get stressed out, whether it was during finals week or when I was getting ready to launch a side hustle, I would remember something that Dale Carnegie used to say. To paraphrase, the most powerful men can be so stressed out that they have to bend down to a little white pill to reduce their stress. But why does it have to be this way? Why couldn't you just remember that in this moment you do not need to be stressed or overwhelmed with anxiety? Ask yourself: Is this one moment going to be important to you five years from now? The answer is almost always no.

That mental exercise has always helped me recenter, find calm, and just focus on the task at hand.

And remember, Beyoncé may have the same number of hours in the day as everyone else, but that doesn't mean all those hours are stress-free. Everyone experiences stress. What matters is how you manage it.

PUSHING FORWARD ALWAYS

People are surprised when they hear that I prefer not to have an assistant. But other than often having my cell phone run out of battery life, I enjoy managing my own schedule. I enjoy being accessible, available. That's why I created Mogul in the first place.

Yeah, when I write it all down, it looks especially difficult. But again, I just take each meeting and each moment as it comes. I often feel so fortunate to be meeting with the companies and people I meet with that that feeling of gratitude overwhelms any feeling of exhaustion. With such high-impact days, you may look back upon the week and not remember anything you did. Because you did so much. But when you work toward a mission—and you realize that just this one day could have helped to create that much more of the change that you want to see in the world—you keep going.

That is being a mogul.

#YouAreAMogul

Figure out what you need to get the best results from your day. Be present at every moment to avoid being overwhelmed by a packed-to-the-brim calendar. We all get the same number of hours in a day, but how you structure those hours can lead to a life of lethargy, a schedule of stress, or a life of boundless energy, excitement, and enthusiasm.

COURTESY OF STARJONES/MARING VISUALS

#IAmAMogul

By Star Jones, attorney, advocate, and original cohost of ABC's *The View*

I want you to know that your success is unlimited. This world will tell you that, because you are a woman, you are limited. Don't believe it.

As a student, you will be told to study one area of interest, declare one major. When you land your first real job, you will be told to climb the ladder and stay there until you retire. And when the time comes, you will be told to choose between having a super-successful career and being an active nurturer for your family. When you have dreams that are too large for most people to understand, you will be told they are "nice" but to make sure you have a backup plan for your impending failure. At every corner, you will face a naysayer, an obstacle, or an internal feeling that you are simply not good enough.

I am here to tell you that it's all lies. You are more than enough!

If your work ethic matches your dreams, there are no limits. You absolutely can work your way up in a company or organization from entry-level to executive, or you can start your own company, write a book, launch a nonprofit—whatever your heart desires. **There are no limitations on your dreams as long as they're backed up by action.** If you have five talents, you can use all five of them. If you have ten dreams, the one that seems the craziest, scariest, and most daring is the one that will succeed. You do not have to choose between career and family, but you will have to choose to align yourself with people and career opportunities that respect the fact that you have a career and a family.

To get through the days that seem hard and discouraging, remember three things:

YOU WILL GET BETTER WITH TIME!

Do not add a projected date to every milestone you hope to reach. No, you will not accomplish all of your life's goals by age twenty-five—maybe not even age thirty-five. You are a fine wine, and age and wisdom will look good on you. Your talent, character, skills, and passions are a journey—not a destination—and will develop over time.

STAY CONNECTED.

The people you connect with will bring you knowledge and countless opportunities. Choose your alignments carefully and never underestimate the value and necessity of a solid personal and professional network.

SUPPORT OTHER WOMEN.

The world will make you think you and other women are competing for the same prize. Social media will have you comparing shades of grass, relationships, success, and dress sizes. Under no circumstances must you accept or participate in this "dog-eat-dog" culture. There is enough success to go around. Supporting other women should be your life's mandate, and you will be happier and widely respected due to your willingness to lift up other women. A rising tide lifts all boats—and as women, we're all in this together.

10 RELY ON YOUR "WHY"

t the end of the day, I didn't create Mogul to make money. I created Mogul to offer opportunities to women: opportunities for connecting, sharing, learning, and growing. I did it to amplify women's voices around the world, so they could express their unfiltered opinions without fear, find community and inspiration, and learn new skills. I did it to honor my family, my parents, for all the sacrifices they made for my siblings and me. I work hard every day to make them proud, to thank them for encouraging me to strive for my full potential, and for showing me that a commitment to others and making the world a better place are truly possible. To me, an empire is not created to amass dollars in the bank, but to create lasting and global impact.

This is my "why."

More and more, we are all demanding jobs that are mission-oriented, that are fulfilling on a personal level and financially rewarding. Adam Neumann, founder of WeWork, says, "We're observing a large generation of amazing individuals being interested in intention and meaning more than material goods." This is largely changing the corporate landscape and the way people work. When your work is personal and fulfilling and driven by more than money, you no longer need a work-life balance.

Work and life begin to fuse together until every moment of your life is just that—life.

The "why" behind Mogul is what keeps me going. No matter how long the days get, when I remember my "why," I'm always reenergized, refocused, and ready to see what other problems Mogul might be able to solve.

It does not matter where you are on your journey. Right now, figure out *"why"* you are going after what you want. Keep that "why" in front of you every step of the way. It will never lead you astray.

SPECIFY YOUR "WHY"

Even if you've never considered your "why," I invite you to move beyond individual motives. How could you, and only you, help us create the changes we need in this world? To be mission-oriented is to be focused on accomplishing something outside of rising in the ranks or pulling in more cash for yourself. It means impacting change in some way, creating hope or opportunity in areas that desperately need it. It can be a global need, like addressing rights for immigrants, or a personal issue, like helping to put your niece through college. But either way, when your "why" involves giving back to others, it pushes you forward and allows you to work harder and longer, because you know your end goal is bigger than yourself.

Sometimes our "why" can start out in broad strokes: wanting to help the environment, or hoping to address lack of opportunity in low-income neighborhoods. But over time, you can home in on how exactly you can help, or the incremental ways you might address a need. After all, Mogul was born from an overall dream to help the countless women across the globe reaching out to me for advice about their personal and professional lives. As I aimed to respond to each new message that came in, I felt strongly that it was important that they have access to the same resources that I had, no matter where they lived. Even more, I wanted them to be able to connect with each other, to realize that when we joined together, we could have a greater impact than we ever could have on our own.

But over time, my "why" came into focus. What was once a broad goal began to evolve into something more specific the longer I worked toward it. I knew that Mogul was uniquely poised to help women, but with so many problems facing women in the world, how *specifically* could it be most impactful?

Early in Mogul's existence, we began to identify the importance of focusing on girls' education. Many cultures still do not value girls' education, refusing access to girls from a very young age. Michelle Obama and the Let Girls Learn initiative publicized the shocking statistic that more than sixty-two million girls were being denied access to education every year. The reasons were varied. Poverty. Forced marriage. Child labor. In some countries, due to lack of social services and orphanages, children were forced to go to prison with their mothers when they were incarcerated (many times not for criminal charges but because they broke cultural taboos). Despite the fact that these children were supposed to be removed from the prisons at age five so that they could receive access to education, many countries did not have the resources to provide care for these children, so they languished in prison, with no exposure to education or the outside world.

It wasn't until an unexpected trip to Austria in 2016 that I became convinced that lack of education for girls was something that Mogul could address and needed to focus on even more. I had been invited to speak at the imperial palace, Hofburg, in Vienna. When I arrived, of the twenty people who had been invited to speak and were present, I was the only woman. Yet I was in awe of my fellow speakers. They had invited royalty from Saudi Arabia; Jimmy Wales, founder of Wikipedia;

Tim Draper, the legendary investor; Ralph Simon, founder of Jive Records; Uma Valeti, founder of Memphis Meats; and Adam Cheyer, creator of Siri—all pioneers who were doing incredible, innovative things, driven by the desire to solve a global issue.

The day before our speeches were to take place, we were flown to an off-site location, where we were locked into a room together, with glass windows all around us as if to literally and figuratively expand our views of the world, and asked the following question: If there was one problem in the world that, when solved, would then solve all other problems in the world, what would that problem be and how would you solve it?

I was sitting in a room with some of the most brilliant minds in the world. The debate was lively, heated, and filled with amazing arguments. Some people thought we needed to address the lack of clean water. Others suggested that we seek to concentrate on famine. Most people's problems were tied to what they were doing in the world, what their enterprise was currently addressing.

I sat there listening. It felt so familiar. Being in a room of men who were older than me. They were all very comfortable adding their voice to the conversation.

I knew that I offered a different perspective, as my solution hadn't been brought up yet. I knew what I needed to say.

Finally, there was a slight pause in the debate.

I worked up the courage in that moment, knowing it was now or never. Despite my hesitation, I knew I would regret it later if I didn't go for it.

Quietly, I said, "If the lack of girls' education was solved, it would solve all other problems."

All nineteen men turned in my direction.

I said it again. This time, a little louder. "If girls across the globe had access to the education they desperately needed, it would solve every other problem."

Even though I could tell that several of the men wanted to question the idea and go back to their own proposed problems, the energy in the room shifted. As we began to debate how many doors this would open, how many more minds we would add to the global conversation, how many more families would be lifted out of poverty, the discussion got more and more lively. This was it. Women needed access to education. And the rest of the world's problems would ultimately be solved. Why? **Because when women are equipped to understand the value that they bring to the world, when they are empowered to realize that they can solve any problem, address any issue, and offer a valuable opinion, then their family, their community, and their whole world will change.**

As the room reached a consensus that girls' education would solve all other issues, the twenty of us then contributed different ideas as to what could help solve the lack of girls' education. When combined, everyone's ideas sounded markedly like the structure behind Mogul.

The final remark before our session ended was: "Well, I guess we should all be investing in Mogul."

And many did.

I knew without a doubt that Mogul could be doing even more to provide access to education. That moment crystallized my "why" in a way that I hadn't felt before. I came back to our HQ more determined than ever. Mogul was offering priceless resources with its Mogul Learning courses. But we knew there were likely many girls who didn't know about Mogul who could benefit from those courses. How could we reach them? How could we stay committed to addressing this problem?

In 2017, we found the answer.

PARTNER TO BROADEN YOUR REACH AND IMPACT

Just a few months after the launch of Mogul, I had been asked to be the closing speaker at an event at Bloomberg through one of our advisors. Despite the many pitches I had made to investors, it was only my second time speaking in public about Mogul (the first was the premiere in Los Angeles), and I was thrilled yet anxious about the opportunity and even more so when a line of people formed to talk to me afterward. One of those people was a woman organizing a forum at the United Nations on diversity and global leadership. She talked to me about the event's purpose and then casually asked whether I might be interested in speaking at it.

I looked at this woman and a chill went down my spine. I remembered how years earlier my father had predicted that this day would come. When I was contemplating quitting my job in finance and taking an unpaid internship at the UN, he had told me to wait. That my time would come. That I would one day be invited to the UN as a guest. This woman had no idea how much her request meant to me. I, of course, accepted, trying to keep my cool, and finished greeting the other people in the line. I then went back to my apartment, where I couldn't wait to tell my parents what had happened.

And on Mogul's one-year anniversary, there I stood at the front microphone, speaking to the rest of the UN chamber, with my name lit up in blue on the screen in front of me. It was a surreal moment. I could have been so nervous, but something came over me. I could feel the excitement from the entire Mogul team, who were all there cheering me on from their seats throughout the UN chamber. I could feel the presence of my mother and father, their unending support, grace, and calm. I hoped they would be proud as I stood on that stage, fulfilling the vision my father had had all those years ago.

It was a wonderful moment to be there, and to share with the UN what Mogul had developed to provide information access, economic opportunity, and education for women worldwide, as well as what our policy recommendations were for gender equity around the world through these facets.

It was the first of many times that I spoke at the UN. A friendship developed naturally with their team as they invited me to return and present more of our work every few months, and I would say yes each time. And as Mogul began to collaborate with the UN Women team more closely we realized that the goals of UN Women were 100 percent aligned with the goals of Mogul. We knew that, by collaborating together, we could ensure a greater reach and impact than either organization could have on its own. In one of our brainstorming sessions, we began to discuss the possibility of a partnership. What if Mogul could provide free access to Mogul Learning—our 1,200 course modules on both personal and professional development—to the very women UN Women was trying to reach and provide education to?

The United Nations is a thorough organization, and it took nine months to formalize our agreement, but on January 13, 2017, we signed the memorandum formalizing our partnership.

And with that, our social impact model was complete: for every dollar that Mogul earned, Mogul would provide free educational resources to one woman in need through international partners such as the United Nations.

It was many years in the making, but it was an amazing moment for all of us. A lot of creative thinking had been needed to mold the relationship in the way that would create the most synergies for all. What were each of our strengths? How could we mitigate each other's weaknesses? These were the questions at the core of our brainstorming sessions. At last, as the partnership came to fruition and young women around the world began to access the courses, it was all well worth the time spent.

When you think about your mission and your ultimate goals, don't be afraid to admit what you are able to do well and what you are not. We can't be good at everything. Think strategically about how you could partner with another organization that could use your resources in order to, when combined with its expertise, truly create exponential reach and impact.

Join Nonprofits for Increased Impact

I encourage you, once you have refined your "why," to think about what nonprofits might be working toward the same mission, and reach out to see how your resources and their expertise might meld together into a partnership of true influence and impact. There are so many people doing so much good in the world, but they need champions and they need resources. Whether you bring monetary resources or marketing reach or just elbow grease, think about how joining with another organization can allow you to make a difference in ways you never thought possible. This also opens the door for a new collaborative relationship and exposure to new people that could lead to opportunities down the road for you, personally and professionally.

IDENTIFY YOUR AREAS OF INFLUENCE

Mogul is not primed to solve every problem in the world. But by homing in on our particular areas of influence, we can see what small part we can contribute. And often the small efforts add up to great impact. This can be true for you. Look at what you are doing and where you could suggest a change, whether it is in your workplace or in your union or in your industry. Sometimes we just need to formalize a request and commitment, and speaking up in that way can lead to an industry's awakening.

Mogul was working hard to address women's access to education, but we knew that wasn't the only facet that held women back globally. There was another issue that we were primed to confront: the need to increase women's share of voice in the world, which still sits at just 10 to 15 percent. This means women pen just 15 percent of op-eds. Just 15 percent of corporate boards are made up of women. I've already covered the statistics of women in government.

Why, when women make up more than 50 percent of the population, and are attending and graduating from college and graduate schools at higher rates than men, are we still faced with a lack of platform?

By encouraging participation and posts on our platform, Mogul allowed women at the earliest stages of their lives to speak up, to share their ideas and insights, to join the conversation and realize their voice and perspective had value.

Mogul Studios was additionally helping to bring women's stories to light in an industry that has often ignored them.

But we began to wonder whether we needed to do more than encourage our clients to responsibly portray women in their ads. In all of our campaigns, there was a certain standard that we always held our clients to. But maybe it was time to formalize that commitment.

I probably don't have to tell you how influential the media and advertising can be for young girls. You've experienced it yourself. You see unrealistic, unattainable standards of beauty, leading to poor body image and low self-esteem. When we are presented with images that suggest that our value lies in our body and how we look, we are disempowered.

Furthermore, women are often portrayed in advertisements in a stereotypical light—the nagging housewife or the sexy siren. In fact, according to the World Economic Forum, women are depicted as intelligent in only 2 percent of advertising. Mogul had been encouraging our partners to commit to showing women in a positive and diverse light. What would happen if little girls were exposed to advertising that showed women in a wide array of positions—as engineers, as pilots, as leaders? Doing this would encourage young women to pursue positions of influence and impact, and also show men how much *more* women could be. "What you see is what inspires your view of what is possible in the world," says Carol Jenkins, president of the Women's Media Center.

These very advertisements could address this lack of voice and encourage our culture to change its outdated views.

It was time for companies to take responsibility for how they could influence positive social change and contribute to the evolution of perceived social standards.

In 2017, I stood again at the podium at the UN, in front of more than three hundred Fortune 1000 chief marketing officers, UN representatives, and reporters. All three hundred people in the room stood and pledged to change the way they marketed to their consumers, and to abide by what we now call the Mogul Standard:

> I pledge to ensure that all marketing and advertising produced by my company will present women in a positive and diverse light in terms of race, physicality, and context, and avoid stereotyping. We stand by efforts to drive positive social change and to reshape the standards that are presented to young girls and women with respect to perceptions of beauty and gender roles.

The UN chamber erupted in a standing ovation.

This could have turned potential clients away, not wanting to be limited by what we would hold them accountable to. But we knew that this was one way we could influence the messages young girls were receiving. And it has been amazing to see the broad support this global initiative has received, as Fortune 1000 CMOs continue to reach out and request to take the pledge to abide by the Mogul Standard.

I truly hope that by demanding this kind of commitment, we will broaden the horizons for young girls, allowing them to see their worth outside of their beauty, aim for positions that have long been attributed to men, and bust out of the boxes that society used to place them in. Katie Couric once said: "Media can be an instrument for change. It can maintain the status quo and reflect the views of the society, or it can hopefully awaken people and change minds. I think it depends on who is piloting the plane."

The world needs us all to be doing our small part to challenge the stereotypes and sexism that for too long have held us back and shut us down. Where is your area of influence? Who are you in contact with, who do you work with, where do you post content? What network are you a part of where you could take a stand and speak up about something that needs to change? **The more we speak up and flood the communication space with positive messages, the more we drown out the noisy, oppressive, and outdated views that attempt to silence us.**

Staying focused on your "why" will allow you to raise your voice, even during times when you feel it may be safer to remain silent.

ALWAYS BE LOOKING FOR A SOLUTION

From a very young age, I have been someone who doesn't want to discuss problems unless we are willing to come up with solutions. I'm not someone who can tolerate much negativity, if it only consists of talking and not doing. I will empathize with you, but then I will always be looking for a solution. Ultimately, that attitude has carried over into Mogul.

In late 2017, as allegations of sexual harassment and assault at the hands of high-profile men throughout different industries came to light, and the #MeToo campaign blazed through social media sites, we at Mogul began to wonder what we could do to address the issues. Being solution-oriented, the offices at Mogul were buzzing as we discussed the comments on the platform and how this was yet one more hurdle that women faced, no matter what industry or what their ultimate goals.

How was it that this kind of behavior had gone unreported for so many years? How had this culture of harassment held women back, as they faced retribution for speaking out, or left organizations because they no longer wanted to face their harasser, giving up opportunities for advancement and economic opportunity? And most important, what could we do to make sure that the culture of silence changed?

The statistics coming to light were discouraging. One out of two women will be harassed at work. Of those, only one in four will report it. The reasons were threefold:

1. Fear of retaliation
2. Fear that the problem wouldn't be addressed even if reported
3. Not knowing where to go to file a report

There was also no mechanism in place for witnesses of harassment to report what they saw. As article after article discussed the problem, very few solutions were being presented.

It clearly wasn't working to have employees report directly to their company's HR reps. We needed some kind of third-party system to monitor complaints. Ashley Judd, one of the whistleblowers, said, "We need to formalize the whisper network. It's an ingenious way that we've tried to keep ourselves safe. All those voices can be amplified." But most nonprofit organizations dedicated to this issue didn't have the resources to create one, and the organizations with resources didn't have missions aligned enough to tackle this problem.

Mogul realized that we were in the unique position to be that third-party organization: we were already a trusted platform for women, and we also had partnerships and relationships with more than twenty thousand HR leaders through our Mogul At Work technologies and were therefore in touch with many of the HR teams at these companies. We were poised to create the very tool the world desperately needed.

So after several weeks of brainstorming sessions, fast-paced meetings, and the creative input of our entire team, Mogul's Safety At Work tool was born. It is a tool that enables the employees of participating companies to be able to log in and file an anonymous report for incidents of assaults and harassment. It is a simple online form that victims or witnesses can fill out. The report automatically goes to multiple HR representatives and stakeholders at that company, which enforces the likelihood that appropriate action is taken. The tool therefore addresses and mitigates each of the issues that previously led to underreporting.

This arose in response to a desperate need that we felt equipped to fulfill. **The world does not just need dreamers, looking to accomplish a goal they set out to attain. The world needs problem solvers, people who will see needs and be willing to address them.**

The driving force at Mogul has always been our "why." Every time we thought about how we might grow the business, we first asked the question: Does it align with our mission? As we began to think about tackling the culture of silence, we didn't even need to ask the question. Of course this aligned with our mission. Because if we could address the rampant sexual harassment, giving victims a way to report abuse and companies an accountability partner to ensure they were addressing this horrendous behavior, it would allow women access to freedom from fear, access to increased opportunity for advancement, and, hopefully, access to more positions of power.

Honestly, we have a lot of work ahead. Until every girl has access to an education, until women are treated fairly in every industry, until every woman is able to walk through the streets without fear of being attacked or is able to express her opinion without fear of being judged strictly because she is a woman, our team will not rest.

Being solution-oriented means that you don't just protest injustice, but you call your senator. You vote on election day. Perhaps you even run for office. Your "why" is the fuel to keep you calling for change and having those difficult conversations because you know that the status quo just isn't going to cut it anymore.

KEEP YOUR "WHY" FRONT AND CENTER

Whether your "why" is global or personal, it helps to come back to it again and again. Why are you sacrificing so much sleep in your side hustles? Because you remember your "why": you want to develop a skill set to be able to achieve your goal. Why are you dealing with so many "nos"? Because you know you will one day get a "yes" that could change your life. Your goal could be anything: you want to become the first female president, or you want to get a promotion by the end of the year. Over time, your "why" will expand when you see how much you can actually accomplish, and you'll want to turn your efforts to something outside yourself. **But keeping that reason, that "why," front and center in your mind allows you to stay energized and focused on what you are trying to accomplish, every step of the way.**

Break It Down

If your "why" ever feels too big, break it down into smaller pieces. The problems we are trying to solve at Mogul are huge, and sometimes the solutions can feel unattainable. But we focus not just globally, but on the individual as well. Anytime I need encouragement,

I simply go onto our site and read about women receiving promotions, getting job offers, getting their Kickstarter funded fully, or starting their own Etsy business thanks to the support they found on Mogul. That reminds me of the "why." That reminds me that, one by one, dream by dream, we are making a difference.

Chelsea Clinton wrote on Mogul: "To be a mogul is to have a vision of something you want to see in the world and get up every day and do what you can to close the gap between where you are and what you want to see." So whether you picked up this book in order to learn how to go after what you want, or make serious money, what I really hope you'll do is realize the power you hold to make a lasting impact.

This is what it means to be a mogul: to see the needs in the world, and to work every day to use your skills, strengths, and resources to address them. Being a mogul means knowing that with your hard work, dedication, and passion, you have what it takes to make the impossible possible.

So don't let anyone convince you to give up on your dreams, or let anything stand in your way. Let this story serve as proof that there's no limit to what you can do.

You are the Mogul the world needs.

#YouAreAMogul

Always remember why you started this journey in the first place. Your "why" can refocus you when you start to lose your way, remind you of how far you have come, and reenergize you to envision what other problems you just might be able to solve.

JULIA RODRIGUES

#IAmAMogul

By Shiza Shahid, founding CEO of the Malala Fund and partner at NOW Ventures

I never could have imagined that this would be my journey. In so many ways, it was all so unlikely.

My story began in Pakistan, where I was born into a humble family. My parents worked hard to give my siblings and me a better life. I grew up in Islamabad, the capital of Pakistan, and was fortunate to have a loving home and access to good schools.

But I was also growing up in a country reeling from poverty, instability, and weak institutions. Pakistan has the second-highest number of children out of school in the entire world. It is ranked the second-worst place to be born a woman.

I wanted to understand the social challenges that plagued the communities around me, so I began volunteering anywhere I could get my foot in the door. When I was thirteen, I volunteered in female prisons, working with an NGO that set up medical camps to help women access health care. When I was sixteen, Pakistan suffered from a devastating earthquake, and I spent the next year volunteering in relief camps to help those who had been most impacted. Even though I was young and untrained, I found ways I could help and just kept showing up.

When I was eighteen, I got a full scholarship to Stanford University, and once again my life changed. Living in Silicon Valley, I was captivated by how new technologies were changing everything. I realized I could harness the power of technology and entrepreneurship to create more scalable solutions to the pressing challenges I had observed back home.

One such challenge was the growing assault on girls' education in remote parts of Pakistan, where terrorist groups were trying to gain power. In my sophomore year, I came across a video about a young Pakistani girl who was committed to getting an education for herself and many young girls like her, despite the rise of terrorism in her hometown that was threatening her access to school. I couldn't believe the courage of this girl, who lived less than three hundred miles from where I grew up, and I reached out to her father to offer my support. We soon decided to run a weeklong camp for his daughter and other young girls, encouraging them to be activists and entrepreneurs, putting them in touch with mentors who could help them in their goal to broaden access to education.

That young girl was Malala Yousafzai, and three years later she was shot by the Taliban for her courage. I was heartbroken and flew in immediately to help her and her family. Thankfully, Malala recovered, and I stayed on to help her and her family share their inspiring story. Together, we started the Malala Fund to help girls around the world access an education. Today, Malala is a Nobel Peace Prize recipient and an amazing young adult, and the Malala Fund is a leading nonprofit in global education.

After serving as the founding CEO of the Malala Fund, I became convinced that the fastest-growing solutions to the world's most pressing challenges were often driven by entrepreneurs with scalable business models rooted in a core innovation, enabled by new technologies. Therefore, I recently launched NOW Ventures, a seed fund that invests in mission-driven startups tackling the world's most critical challenges. **The question I ask myself when I invest is: If this idea succeeds, how will the world be a fundamentally better place?**

I try to always remain driven by a core set of passions, which I have felt since I was a child. I constantly ask myself: What makes me come alive? If I had one year to live, what work would I still choose to do? I remind myself not to be driven by fear, but by hope. I am grateful for all the work I have gotten to do, the wonderful people I've met along the way, the adventures, and even the heartbreak that has led me here today.

MOGUL
MANTRAS

'm thankful you took the time to read about what I've learned (and all the glorious challenges and triumphs along the way). More than anything, I hope that you take what you've learned in this book and apply it to what you have always dreamed of doing today. Now is the moment to take your life into your own hands. Do the impossible, do it yourself, and do it now.

To continue guiding you, below are a few phrases that have always kept me going, during even the most challenging days. Go ahead and take a screenshot with your phone, or rip these pages out of this book and post them on your bathroom mirror or place them on your bedside table, in your cubicle, or anywhere else you may need inspiration. Remember these truths, and remember always: you are a mogul.

You've got to kill it and over-deliver on every task you are given.

———————

You cannot leave promotions and raises to chance. You must be proactive about them and ask. It's important to be in charge of your own destiny.

———————

If your day job isn't your passion, use those extra hours to discover what it is you truly love to do.

———————

If you are only willing to work during your office hours, you miss out on opportunities for so many fulfilling endeavors, and the ability to start having an impact now.

———————

When you build trust and become someone's go-to person for any job, big or small, you can accelerate your path to the job you truly want.

———————

True failure is turning away from opportunity because you don't want to face your fear.

———————

When you dare to try something new, it can be the opening of the door that leads to everything you've always wanted.

———————

Rapidly prototype and iterate toward perfection over time.
Whatever the idea may be, just get started. The hard part is
often just beginning, no matter what you're trying to do.

———————

The choices that we make in our romantic lives are just as important
to our eventual success as the choices we make in our careers.

———————

Always be kind, be authentic, be generous.
Be willing to go the extra mile.

———————

When you learn how to comfortably mesh who you are in your
professional life with who you are in your personal life, you
enable yourself to be the most authentic version of yourself.

———————

Always envision that with all your hard work and dedication, the
best scenario could happen. The impossible is actually possible.

———————

A "no" is a "not right now" that will turn into a "yes." There
will come a day when those who initially said "no" to you
will come chasing after you, in disbelief at your success.

———————

It does not matter where you are on your journey. Right now, figure
out *why* you are going after what you want. Keep that "why" in
front of you every step of the way. It will never lead you astray.

———————

Now, one final thing.

It's your turn to share your #IAmAMogul.

What's your story?

ACKNOWLEDGMENTS

I want to thank Cindy DiTiberio, Jill Grinberg, Denise St. Pierre, and Sophia Seidner for being the most incredible, loyal, passionate, dedicated collaborators I could have ever hoped for. Thank you for all the late nights, calls, emails, text messages, and teas over these past two years. This book became magnificent because of your magnificence.

Thank you to Christine Pride, Jonathan Karp, Michele Martin, and Diana Ventimiglia for believing in us and our collaboration. You recognized that this was a movement.

Thank you to my incredible father and mother, as well as my wonderful brother, David, and sister, Kym, for supporting and contributing to each idea, each concept, found within this book. There were so many late nights of writing and editing where our family's love and laughter pulled me through. David, thank you especially for reading draft after draft and contributing your thoughts to every new paragraph written, after every edit (even this one). Your unending support and wisdom remain unmatched.

I am thankful for my best friends Stephanie Bartz, Lauren Wasserman, Maya Farah, Diane Shao, Susannah Bragg, Aubrie Pagano, Chrissie Gorman, Lizzi Ackerman, Tina Mashaalahi, Erik Woelber, Jason Burinescu, and Krystal Bowden, for messaging me constant support and endless GIFs on Facebook Messenger to cheer me on.

To our incredible team members at Mogul, you represent the love and passion behind everything we do. Thank you to Juli Szaller, Namisha Bahl, Natasha Birnbaum, Bethany Heinrich, and everyone else on our team for your unending belief in our mission, as well as your ongoing offers to help on this project.

And most of all, thank you to our Mogul users: our amazing women, students, influencers, advisors, investors, and think tank members from across the world. This book was born from you, for you. We would not be where we are today without you.

ABOUT THE AUTHOR

AUDREY FROGGATT

TIFFANY PHAM is the founder and CEO of Mogul, one of the largest platforms for women worldwide to connect, converse, and access knowledge from one another. A coder, she developed the first version of Mogul, which now reaches millions of women across 196 countries through its mobile app, the web, email, social media, books, TV, films, and events. Tiffany was named one of *Forbes*'s "30 Under 30" in media, *Business Insider*'s "30 Most Important Women Under 30" in technology, *ELLE Magazine*'s "30 Women Under 30 Who Are Changing the World," *Good Housekeeping*'s Awesome Women Award Winner, Cadillac's IVY Innovator Award Winner, *SmartCEO Magazine*'s Smart CEO Award Honoree, an Alice Paul Equality Award Honoree, Digital Diversity Network's Innovation & Inclusion Award for Social Entrepreneurship Honoree, a Tribeca Disruptive Innovation Awards Fellow, and *New York Business Journal*'s Woman of Influence. Tiffany is a judge on the TLC TV show *Girl Starter* and is a regular speaker at the United Nations. She is the coauthor of *From Business Strategy to Information Technology Roadmap: A Practical Guide for Executives and Board Members*, and is a graduate of Yale and Harvard Business School.